WITCHCRAFT
AND PAGANISM
TODAY

WITCHCRAFT AND PAGANISM TODAY

Anthony Kemp

Brockhampton Press

London

First published in Great Britain in 1993
Michael O'Mara Books Limited
9 Lion Yard
Tremadoc Road
London SW4 7NQ

A CIP catalogue record for this book is
available from the British Library.

This edition published 1995 by Brockhampton Press,
a member of Hodder Headline PLC Group

ISBN 1 86019 127 4

Printed and bound in Great Britain by
BPC Hazell Books Ltd
A member of
The British Printing Company Ltd

❦ Contents ❦

❦ Foreword ❦

For many people the word Witchcraft is associated with pointed hats, warty noses and broomsticks. An entire industry has grown up around Hallowe'en to perpetuate these myths, and at that season even the most staid are happy to dress up in supposedly occult costumes. For others, the subject raises an irrational fear of the unknown, on which the popular press has seized, promoting sexual titillation which borders on obscenity. A headline such as 'I was Satan's Sex Slave' is a sure way of grabbing readers' attention, especially if coupled with details of a naked virgin being sacrificed on an altar in a council house in Milton Keynes. For many Christians, particularly fundamentalists, Witchcraft is seen as Satan's work, corrupting the nation's morals. Yet if you enter any bookshop today, you will find the section entitled 'Mysticism' or 'Occult' three times as large as that stocking mainstream religious literature. Either a large section of the population is genuinely seeking new knowledge or the nation is on the path to a moral decay.

Recently the alleged 'ritual abuse' of children has occupied the attention of the courts. These cases encouraged the public to assume that Satanic forces were at large within society. But the cases collapsed, exposed as an exercise in mass hysteria engineered by American-based fundamentalist Christian sects who exploited gullible social workers, and the very real anxiety about the exposure of young people to video films of the nastier sort. In the popular press Witchcraft has always been an easy target because of its lack of organisation and credible spokespersons. Yet this misrepresents many ordinary people who follow a religion based on love and respect for Nature, including all human life. Today various re-creations of ancient Pagan beliefs are increasing in popularity, notably among young people, and their adherents claim that they have much to teach us about practical methods of safeguarding the environment for our children. All that they ask for is tolerance, based on the legal right to freedom of worship enshrined in international treaties.

My own background combines military experience and a degree in history, which led me into journalism. With the exception of the muscular Christianity instilled in me at my public school, my attitude to religion remained neutral. I encountered Witchcraft by chance and initially with much scepticism. For several years I was employed as a researcher and producer in the factual programmes department of one of the Independent Television contractors. There was a sensational 'Satanism' trial in our area in the south of England in which the defendant had relieved a number of worthies of considerable sums of money. As the word Witchcraft had been bandied about, I was asked to prepare a background piece. I set off into unknown territory without any preconceived notions. For a number of reasons my research was never used, but I retained a close interest in the subject. Since then I have continued what has become a personal voyage of discovery, have enjoyed the company of many sincere and loving people, have read half a library of books and have met a number of fools and crackpots. One could, of course, say the same about research into any branch of religion.

Many of those who I might wish to thank for their guidance must remain anonymous or cloaked by pseudonyms. Sadly there is still the ever-present danger of having one's windows smashed or being discriminated against at work or socially if one admits to being a witch. My gratitude, however, must go to Debbie, Priestess of Hathor, who managed to convince me many years ago that it was not all bunkum, and to Sara of the Priory of Saint Brighid, who helped me to understand. With Ayla, Constance and 'K' I was able to tread the spiral dance most wonderfully. I offer, too, my respect and admiration to Alex Rosenberger and his companions who have tirelessly campaigned to gain access to Stonehenge for the Summer Solstice and as a result have suffered from the attentions of the Wiltshire Constabulary. Anybody interested in Paganism owes a great deal to those who have steered the Pagan Federation out of the waters of factional strife and into the respected position it enjoys today. Finally I would like to thank Doreen Valiente, to whom this book is dedicated, for her wit, her wisdom, her poetry and her plain common sense about a subject which so many persist in regarding as evil.

❦ Introduction ❦

It is early evening somewhere in Britain and a handful of people are arriving outside an ordinary house in a typical street of modest dwellings. They come as couples or alone, by car, bicycle or on foot, and are carrying bottles of wine or bowls of food to share. Their way to the door is lit by the street lamps and the pale gentle light of a full moon in the clear sky overhead. They are admitted by a woman wearing a loose kaftan-like dress who greets each one with a kiss and the words 'Blessed Be'. Bottles and food are left in the kitchen and the guests assemble in the lounge, chatting easily with one another and their hostess, making jokes about those who are habitually late. It could almost be the start of a local Tupperware party.

The room in which they are sitting is furnished conventionally. Yet there are subtle differences. In one corner there is a small table covered by a cloth on which is a lighted candle, a figurine of a naked woman and a vase of flowers. Those present, about a dozen in all, are

1

dressed like any cross-section of the community, although the women tend to wear silver jewellery and loose dresses rather than the latest in High Street fashion. When everyone has arrived, the hostess indicates that they should start and there is a scramble to move the furniture, to leave an open space in the centre of the room. The small cloth-covered table is placed in the north and various extra objects are laid out on it. A candle is positioned at each cardinal point of the room and at the last minute someone remembers to unplug the telephone.

Then in ones and twos they move upstairs into one of the bedrooms and get undressed, piling their clothes on the bed. Some who have not had time beforehand take a quick shower in the bathroom. There is no embarrassment as all are at ease with each other in their nakedness and can laugh and talk together. Each one binds a cord around his or her waist and produces a black-handled knife from pocket or bag. Moving off down the stairs they enter the candle-lit living room where their hostess and her partner are waiting for them. She is standing before the small table, naked and with her hair streaming down her back, her womanness emphasised by a necklace and a silver headband bearing the symbol of the crescent moon. She may be a civil servant or work for a bank, but in that place and at that time she is the high priestess of the ancient Moon Goddess, Queen of the circle and witch. The rite can begin.

That same scene, with minor variations, will be taking place all over the country on the night of every full moon as the followers of the old religion gather to celebrate their beliefs. They call their religion Wicca and often refer to themselves, both male and female, as witches. No virgins are ravished on the altar, no children are present and no livestock ritually slaughtered.

Afterwards they will have a bit of a party, dress and go home ready for work the next day. If we are to believe the popular press, these people are child abusers, Satanists and evildoers, celebrating the Black Mass and indulging in all sorts of obscene abominations. It is, however, a fact that popular interest in occultism in all its forms, and in alternative religions, therapies and lifestyles, is greatly on the increase in Britain, although this phenomenon is consistently misunderstood.

The aim of this book is to present as complete a picture as possible of the Pagan revival in modern Britain and particularly to examine the beliefs and practices of the Wiccan religion. In doing so I hope that some misunderstandings can be cleared up and some informed opinion presented without prejudice. Numerous books about Wicca or the Craft have appeared in recent years but have mainly been written by adherents wishing to promote their own particular brand of belief. Often they only perpetrate misconceptions, as is the case with all religions. After all, the historical person of Jesus of Nazareth was vastly different from the version conveyed over the centuries by the various Christian churches. Pagans themselves feel that they are gravely misunderstood and badly treated by the media. In her recent book *Voices from the Circle*, which she co-edited with Prudence Jones, Caitlin Matthews wrote of their experiences with a BBC radio programme. 'Although all contributors had given positive and stimulating interviews, stressing the beneficial and spiritual aspects of the diverse Pagan traditions, the programme's editor had cut the tape together to include interviews from hard-line clergy and hearsay on the negative aspects of Paganism, specifically witchcraft, on certain unbalanced individuals. This material, inserted with no right of reply, made all those interviews sound suspect, if not downright evil.'

The journalistic approach to the Pagan revival alternates between outright condemnation and the poking of fun at those whose enjoyment of dancing in a circle and making merry is seen as an automatic sign of lunacy. This is the type of writing that revels in broomsticks and pointed hats and focuses on what might be called 'Rentawitch', a small number of self-publicists who enjoy the limelight and will give an interview at the drop of a black cloak. Paganism is thus treated as an archaism in the materialistic twentieth century and as the harmless pursuit of a small number of head cases.

In spite of its popular image as an evil spiritual force or lunatic fringe activity, Paganism in its various forms is enjoying an ever-increasing level of support and a large number of people derive spiritual fulfilment from such beliefs.

Before delving more deeply into the subject, it is necessary to establish a few basic definitions to form a frame of reference. The word 'occult' literally means hidden and covers many activities and beliefs that are not necessarily religious in character: among them are astrology, fortune-telling, dowsing, magical systems such as the Hebrew Kabbalah, certain aspects of alternative medicine, Theosophy, Anthroposophy and Witchcraft.

Paganism is derived from the Latin word *pagani*, which literally means 'country dwellers', although it is popularly misused to describe unbelievers. Those who profess Paganism, however, see themselves as followers of a nature-based tradition that never truly disappeared in Europe. Its revival owes much to breaking down of old taboos during the 1960s and the growing awareness of potential ecological disaster. Pagans argue that the world's major religions have not shown a responsible attitude towards the natural resources of the planet and that theirs is the only true 'Green' belief. The Pagan

Federation, a loosely organized but nevertheless responsible body which unites the various traditions in Britain,
lays down three principles which any potential member
must first accept:

1. *Love for and kinship with Nature*, rather than the
more customary attitude of aggression and domina-
tion over Nature. Reverence for the life force, and
the continuing renewing cycle of life and death.

2. *The Pagan Ethic*, 'Do what thou will, but harm
none'. This is a *positive* morality, not a list of thou-
shalt-nots. Each person is responsible for discovering his or her own true nature and developing it
fully in harmony with the world around them.

3. *Acceptance of the polarity of deity*, the reality of both
Goddess and God. Active participation in the cosmic
dance of Goddess and God, female and male, rather
than the suppression of either the male or the
female principle.

Perhaps only the more bigoted members of the
orthodox religions could find anything harmful in
these principles. The Pagan world in Britain encom-
passes a number of strands such as Druidism, Nordic
beliefs, followers of North American Indian shamanism,
Oriental mysticism and the various branches into which
Wicca or Witchcraft is divided. All Witches are Pagans,
but not all Pagans are Witches. Paganism regards itself
as a religion without strict dogma and divided, like most
others, into differing branches or sects. In a statement
on Modern Paganism issued recently, the authors state
that 'Paganism aims to offer a way to recognize and
attune oneself to the manifold forces of Nature, which
already exist within and without us, and which are vital
to our survival, fulfilment and evolution. By celebrating

the seasons and becoming one with other living creatures, Pagans synchronize intimately with the planet,
and liberate their personalities and magnify their per-
ception and talents in the interests of themselves, their
groups and communities, and humankind as a whole.'

Although there is some evidence that small pockets of
traditional Witchcraft survived in Britain through the
centuries, the popular religion that has developed from
it is a creation or a reinvention dating from the 1950s.
In 1951 the last remaining statutes concerning
Witchcraft were repealed and a man called Gerald
Gardner published a book in which he revealed some of
his own views on the subject. He went on to found a
coven and called his new movement Wicca. As he
enjoyed quite a high public profile, his ideas had an
instant appeal for many people and subsequently have
been spread all over the world. Although Gardner laid
down a basis for the rituals used, they have been adapted in many ways to suit personal needs. Today there are
countless versions of Wicca, all of which, nonetheless,
have many features in common.

It is essential to bear in mind that neither Paganism
nor Witchcraft has anything in common with Satanism
or devil-worship. Pagans do not accept the existence of
the devil, regarding him as a Christian aberration, and
thus cannot worship him. The fact that some people do
so is an undeniable fact, but the Pagan world can hardly
be blamed. By the same token the much-quoted Black
Mass is a Christian perversion. In theory, to celebrate
it, you need a de-frocked Roman Catholic priest and
the ability to gabble the Latin mass backwards while
defecating on the Christian symbols and books. Quite
what that exercise is meant to achieve is difficult to
understand, except perhaps to give ex-Christians a
chance to vent their spleen on the church.

Black magic is a totally different matter. Anyone who believes in the power of magic, and has the ability to execute it, has the choice between black and white working. If, however, that person consciously chooses to do evil, he will run foul of the old natural law of three-fold return, which states that evil will return with triple force against the person who originated it.

The most persistent accusation levelled against Witches is their supposed involvement in child abuse. This unfounded charge came to the fore in 1988. A series of sensational articles in the press stated that young girls were being used as brood-mares to provide babies for ritual sacrifice; that children were being forced to witness terrible perversions; and that numerous people were being driven mad by Witches. Behind this campaign were an organization known as Childwatch, the Conservative Member of Parliament, Geoffrey Dickens, and a number of clergy-men. The *Sunday Mirror* of 30 October 1988 ran a headline reading 'Babies Sacrified to Satan', and under-neath 'Mothers forced to watch slaughter of innocents at black magic rituals'. It emerged that these allegations referred to a case in North America, yet the woman who runs Childwatch claimed that such activities were happening in Britain. Nevertheless, no hard and fast evidence of these activities has ever been presented, and abuses which have been shown to have taken place have been the work of paedophiles. The fact that these perverts may dress up in robes testifies to the fact that they enjoy sadistic videos; it does not make them Witches. Pagan parents argue that the orthodox religions are themselves guilty of child abuse. Why is there no outcry against the ritual mutilation of small boys who because of the fact that they have been born into Muslim or Jewish families, have their foreskins forcibly removed when they are not old enough to give their permission freely?

The recent collapse of the Rochdale, Orkney and Epping Forest ritual child abuse cases highlighted the fact that an irrational fear of the occult and Witchcraft persists in Britain, fuelled by some sections of the media, a couple of MPs and the battalions of fundamentalist Christianity. Misguided social workers jumped to the wrong conclusions, and as a result a number of families were torn apart. Yet a visit to any video hire shop will demonstrate that a large variety of shoddily produced semi-pornographic films, dealing with sacrifices to the devil, robed high priests and mysterious sexually oriented rituals, are readily available on the shelves. Script writers have pillaged the novels of Dennis Wheatley for stimulation and have simply rehashed the same old cocktail of perversion in the guise of entertainment. If it is all so terrible, why do people watch it?

Child abuse, whether physical, sexual or mental, is nothing new. Previously it was often thought of as the work of a 'wicked stranger', but in many recent cases the guilty parties have been shown to be members of the child's immediate family. Any abuse of children is an abomination, but any attempt to fix the blame on a particular section of the community clouds the issue. The campaign to prove that witches are child abusers originated in the United States and then spread into Europe, where it was enthusiastically embraced by some sections of the Evangelical movement. A plethora of organisations such as the Reachout Trust, Christian Response to the Occult, the Deo Gloria Trust and Childwatch jumped on to the well-funded band-waggon with shattering results for a large number of children and their families. Seminars were held by supposed 'expert' lecturers and attended by social workers, teachers and members of the police, at which the myth of Satanic abuse was planted into untutored minds. At the same time the media was bombarded with material which many journalists accepted at face value. The final straw came in April 1988 when Mr Geoffrey Dickens, the MP for Littleborough and Saddleworth called for a debate in Parliament on the subject of witchcraft which he felt should be banned.

The recently proclaimed Decade of Evangelism has declared open war on the occult, prompting fears that a new wave of persecution is about to be launched against the Pagan community. Every year during October the press is bombarded with anti-Hallowe'en propaganda and dutifully prints it. Tabloid newspapers regale their readers with tales of Satanic rites, orgies and nakedness, proclaiming such activities to be evil, yet shamelessly titillating their readership at the same time. Paradoxically these same newspapers are also full of stories about scout leaders, choir masters and vicars who have taken an indecent interest in their young charges. In 1990 there were reports of eight Christian ministers being convicted of the sexual abuse of children. No sensible person would claim as a result that all Christian youth workers are paedophiles, so why is it assumed that all witches are automatically evil? Ironically, the press criticism is usually counterproductive. In one of her books Doreen Valiente wrote: 'Every time there is a big "exposure of the evils of witchcraft" in the sensational Press, it is followed by sackfuls of letters from people wanting to know how they can join a coven!'

Article No. 18 of the Universal Declaration of Human Rights, passed by the United Nations, states:

Everyone has the right to freedom of thought, conscience and religion; this right includes freedom to change his religion or belief, and freedom, either alone or in community with others and in public or in private, to manifest his religion or belief in teaching, practice, worship and observance.

In June 1989. Alex Rosenberger, a leading activist in the movement for free access to Stonehenge for the celebration of the Summer Solstice, was arrested at the entrance to Salisbury Cathedral for reading out the above declaration.

Curiously, the newspaper readers who are simultaneously shocked and fascinated by exposures of the evils of witchcraft retain an insatiable appetite for spurious occultism. They will avidly read their 'stars' while at the same time proclaiming that astrology is a lot of rubbish; consult palmists at fairgrounds; and keep a whole army of clairvoyants in business. You can even get a supposedly 'personal' Tarot reading by telephone and purchase a horoscope that has been prepared by a computer programme. Popular superstition accepts that it is lucky if a black cat crosses your path or if you find a four-leafed clover. There are two ways of looking at these phenomena. Either the public is extremely gullible or, as a nation, we are at heart Pagans who have subconsciously clung to the Old Religion in spite of centuries of Christianity. After all, we celebrate the birth of Jesus of Nazareth in Palestine, which probably happened in the Spring, with all the trappings of the Pagan Winter Solstice, including mistletoe, holly and feasting.

Pagan folk are human beings, subject to all the frailties and foibles that enrich society. I hope that this book will make the point that they have something positive to offer and should not be considered a menace which threatens the nation's morals. The reader may not necessarily accept their views or attitudes to life, but the fact remains that there are quite a lot of them around.

❦ 1 ❦
The Historical Background

The modern practitioners of what is termed Witchcraft, or Wicca, refer to their beliefs as the Old Religion and claim to worship the Old Gods. Much of their ethos is based upon their belief that the ancient religion of Britain survived through the centuries of persecution as an oral tradition, although it must be said there is little evidence of this. Gerald Gardner who produced the *Book of Shadows* in which the practices of the Craft are laid down was fascinated by pseudo-medieval language and was fond of references to the times of the persecutions. One of his basic beliefs was that Witchcraft continued to exist and he said that he had been initiated into a coven operating in the New Forest.

Modern Druidry also claims an ancient pre-Christian lineage. In the wider Pagan community there is much anger that the Druids have been deprived of the right to worship at Stonehenge on the morning of the Summer Solstice. This contemporary evocation of a mythical golden age in the past characterizes the yearnings of many people who feel threatened by modern technology and the depersonalization of society. The popular fascination with fantasy tales such as Tolkien's *Lord of the Rings* and in role-playing games such as Dungeons and Dragons is evidence of these feelings. Faced with a drab daily existence, increasingly large numbers of people seek an escape in imaginary role-playing in which, wielding magic swords and guided by ancient wizards, they set out to rescue maidens and wrest treasure from monsters. The rise in the acceptance of neo-Pagan religious views is one aspect of the failure of both modern technological society and the declining Christian churches to provide food for the psyche.

Examination of the practices of the various Pagan groupings in Britain today reveals that they incorporate strands from a number of occult traditions and patterns of belief. The adherents of all religions firmly avow that their particular brand of faith is the only one and that their God is the best. Thus faiths which have much in common have continued to divide the human race, frequently with baleful results. Underlying the main-stream religions, however, runs a hidden seam of centuries-old knowledge which has been disguised from the prying minds of the inquisitors. It is from this occult tradition that modern Paganism stems, rather than from eccentric old ladies brewing herbs in cottage cauldrons.

The human psyche has an inbuilt need to acknowledge the supernatural. There are those who claim to be atheists, but they are rare and their supposed lack of belief is often only a cloak for self-doubt. From the earliest time, human beings have sought to explain the mysteries of where they came from and where they would go when they died in terms of myths and legends, which were adapted and altered as societies changed. The Gods and Goddesses, warriors, heroes and demons created by our ancestors were merely aspects of certain essential truths common to all. As nations were conquered, their Gods and Goddesses were frequently incorporated in the pantheons of the new masters, happily settling alongside those already there. It was the rise of the monotheistic religions, with their notion of a single all-wise God, who gave his believers the right to wipe out all potential rivals, which produced so much human misery. It took centuries, and heaps of dead bodies, for Christianity finally to triumph over Paganism in Europe, yet today the Churches are in decline and an interest in the old beliefs is resurgent.

Primitive man was preoccupied with gathering and hunting sufficient food to ensure the survival of his social group. The world in which he found himself was full of terrors and death lurked around every corner. The awe-inspiring powers of nature had to be placated, as there was then no easy scientific explanation of such phenomena as earthquakes and volcanoes. As the members of a small hunting band took shelter from a raging thunderstorm, cowering together in a cave, it was natural to believe that the Gods were angry. Close as they were to nature, those early humans developed an understanding of the yearly seasonal cycle upon which they depended for their lives. Surviving early Stone Age cave paintings in southern France prove the artistic ability of our most distant ancestors as well as showing human forms dressed in animal skins. By taking on the spirit of an animal, it was believed that the hunter could exert an influence on the outcome of the chase.

In spite of the relentless efforts by modern missionaries to stamp out such heathen practices, similar beliefs exist today among African tribes, the Aboriginals in

Australia and in many other less developed countries. They are usually classified as primitive, but as they live in a close relationship with nature, such societies cause far less environmental damage than the supposedly civilised ones. Crucial to their religious thinking is a concern with animal and human fertility, without which the tribe could not survive. Early in the history of human development came the idea of a female deity, the Earth Mother, who was linked to the Moon by her own monthly cycle. She could not function, however, without the fertilizing aspect of the male, which in turn was likened to the power and warmth of the Sun. Sun and Moon together ruled over night and day and the yearly seasonal changes. Thus the Mother gained a consort, the Hunter God depicted with horns and often in semi-animal form.

Tribal societies, aware of their dependence on the forces of Nature, sought to communicate with them and placate them with sacrifices. By a process of natural evolution, it became obvious that certain individuals had more ability in establishing contact, and thus the witch-doctor or shaman made an appearance. Rites were developed to suit the particular needs of the tribe, such as ancestor worship, initiation at puberty, seasonal festivals and birth and marriage. Many of these ideas have been carried into modern times by the established religions and are part and parcel of the neo-Pagan movement.

Around 4,000 BC civilization took a great leap forward with the development of highly sophisticated city states, both in Egypt and in the Tigris-Euphrates Delta. To satisfy the needs of urban societies, complicated religions evolved served by an educated priestly caste which occupied itself with the beginnings of scientific enquiry. Astronomy and Astrology were used as the basis for calculation of planetary movements and seasonal variations. The annual flooding of the Nile, for example, was vital for the survival of Egyptian life and the ability to predict and influence that event became an important religious function.

In many sections of the occult world there is a belief that the development of urban civilization come about as the result of extra-terrestrial intervention. This view has been popularized by the books of Erich von Däniken. Using snippets of ancient legends and the evidence of surviving structures, von Däniken has sought to prove that spacemen had visited the Earth and taught men a variety of skills. As a result, the visitors became identified with Gods and tapestries of myth were woven around their deeds. Associated with this concept is the ancient controversy about Atlantis, the mythical island which sank beneath the Atlantic. This has been portrayed as a veritable paradise on earth, populated by a race of superbeings endowed with the knowledge of the great cosmic secrets.

There may be some truth in these ideas. The Biblical legend of the flood, for example, might have its origins in a global catastrophe that wiped out Atlantis. Nevertheless, attempts to explain religious development in terms of extra-terrestrial influence remain pure speculation. It is from that period, however, that belief changed. On the one hand, primitive societies clung to the worship of nature deities and continued to practise the rites associated with tribal fertility. On the other, larger state systems equipped with the ability to communicate in writing developed a body of knowledge based on accurate observation. An educated priestly caste serving the needs of rulers who were often priest kings monopolized this knowledge in order to maintain their own power and privileges. Some of this information was preserved, however, and has been handed down through cultured and literate elites. It is from these two strands that modern Paganism derives its beliefs.

Although we know very little about the details of Celtic religious observance, many of the tribal customs of our ancestors have survived into the present day, in spite of Christian attempts to eradicate them. Easter eggs, maypoles, the dressing of wells and the carrying of green boughs into the churches in spring are examples now simply classified as folklore. The Old Gods did not disappear; they went underground but remained in the consciousness of the people.

A variety of cultural elements gave native British paganism its particular frame of reference. Firstly, in pre-Roman times, there were the Celtic peoples, worshipping a variety of deities which were served by an order of priests and teachers known as the Druids. The Celts had suppressed the older inhabitants of the islands who had built the stone circles, pressing the survivors into the western extremities of Britain. Then the Celtic peoples of Britain were subjugated by the Romans, who brought their own religion which co-existed with the local pantheon of deities. With the departure of regular Roman troops in 410 AD, the inhabitants had to come to grips with regular waves of Norse invaders who introduced their own myths and legends and a new Pantheon of warrior Gods and Goddesses. Inevitably there was intermingling and the struggle between the two cultures for supremacy spawned a new crop of legends. From these sprang the legend of the mystical leader Arthur and the rich pattern of romance woven around his court at Camelot. The so-called Dark Ages were not so dark as many believe and wandering story tellers spread the legends from settlement to settlement, embellishing them through the generations. Lingering folk memories of the ancient peoples dispossessed by the Celts produced the tales of the fairy folk or the little people, who were skilled in sorcery and had to be placated by offerings. Such customs remain in rural Ireland today in spite of centuries of Catholicism.

In Britain Christianity had an uphill struggle to gain acceptance. The beliefs of the Celtic Church which emerged in the fifth century were at variance with those of the Roman papacy which had to send a mission led by Augustine to Britain. In an illiterate age the one great advantage possessed by the Church was a universal written language, Latin, and an educated priesthood. Gradually the various petty rulers were won over, although many of them only paid lip-service to the new beliefs when the priest was around. Christianity could not co-exist with Paganism and the vicious cycle of licensed persecution began wherever the newcomers gained a toe-hold. The Horned God of the country folk became the devil and the desexualised Mary took over from the fecund Celtic Goddesses. Churches were built on Pagan sites, the Druids were slaughtered and their sacred groves were cut down. By the ninth century Britain was nominally within the greater Christian fold, although allegiance to Rome remained a permanent irritant to its rulers until Henry VIII declared his independence.

After the Battle of Hastings in 1066, much of the native aristocracy of Celtic and Norse ancestry was either killed or fled abroad. The new Norman masters spoke no English and imposed their rule from the castles they built throughout the land. The Celtic fringe, however, managed to hold out and preserve what was left of its language and culture for many centuries. What we do not know is the extent to which native Paganism actually survived. There is no evidence of any organized alternative religion, although it is clear that at village level the wise woman or the cunning man was still consulted in matters of healing, love potions and even putting a curse on the neighbour's cattle. In France today the local midwife is officially known as a *sage femme*, a wise woman. At the traditional times of the year, the peasants went off into the woods to worship the old Horned God and indulge in a bit of merry fertility. Parallel to this, the more civilized of the aristocracy continued to enjoy the old tales in the castle hall which had simply been given a Christian gloss.

The Middle Ages were a period of turmoil, of doubt, of rebellion against authority and intellectual curiosity. On the surface the Church was triumphant, but in reality it was frequently on the defensive. The clergy were generally regarded as the corrupt allies of a ruling class which exploited the suffering peasantry to finance its wars and luxurious lifestyles. The Crusaders returned from the Middle East with dangerous ideas and copies of Greek and Roman philosophical texts. Periodically old heresies resurfaced and a small-time local bandit operating in Sherwood Forest was elevated to the status of popular folk-hero, invested with many of the attributes of the old forest God.

The Inquisition was founded in the thirteenth century to combat heresy. For a century it concentrated on the suppression of mass heretical movements in continental Europe. Then an oppressive eye was turned on the remnants of Paganism which flourished among country folk. Pennethorne Hughes has described the beliefs of these Pagans, after 600 years of Christianity, as 'a jumble of phallic Druidism, the dregs of Mediterranean ritual, Scandinavian magic, and, before long, Christian parody'. The problem is that the only real evidence we possess comes from the records of the inquisitors, who were naturally biased and extracted their confessions under torture. Unlettered, simple people were fed loaded questions designed to produce the answers required. The result resembled the state trials under Stalin in which the guilt of the accused was assumed and the sentence a foregone conclusion. Underlying the exaggerations, however, there is a strand of knowledge which enables us to gain an insight into the workings of traditional witchcraft.

Persecution swept across Britain and Europe in waves as the Church whipped up popular antagonism against witches and fairies, as they were ofen named. The Jews suffered equally from this persecution; the accusation of ritual sacrifice of children often made against them was also levelled against Pagans. The basic charge was heresy in that such deluded folk consorted with and worshipped the devil. Initially, the Christians had it all their own way, but after the Reformation of the sixteenth century, the Protestants went witch-hunting with even more venom. It became easy to denounce a neighbour to the authorities by claiming that he or she — usually it was a she — had made your cattle miscarry or had blighted your crops. Gerald Gardner, the founder of modern witchery claimed that nine million witches had perished. He had no evidence for arriving at this figure but the number was certainly considerable.

In late-medieval and early Tudor England, the relatively small number of prosecutions generally resulted from a charge of sorcery rather than the fact that the accused was a witch. The worst excesses were on the continent of Europe where mass hysteria was used to whip up popular feeling against anyone who could even remotely be accused of any form of deviant behaviour. In 1490, two Dominican priests, Sprenger and Krämer, wrote a pamphlet, entitled the *Malleus Maleficarum*, which became the Bible of witch persecution, laying down such matters as how to identify a witch. Read today it is laughable were it not for the fact that it resulted in the horrible deaths of thousands of individuals.

The authorities in Elizabethan England had a more relaxed attitude to witchcraft, although many Protestant clergy who had been exiled during the reign of Mary (1516–58) returned home full of morbid Calvinist witch-mania. It was in the reign of Elizabeth's successor, however, that serious persecution began. Before coming to the throne in 1603, James I as King of Scotland had published a book, *Daemonologie*, and was attended by a clergy imbued with the hatred of witchcraft endemic on the Continent. In his first Bill before Parliament, witchcraft *per se* was made punishable by death for the first time. A wave of persecution followed, with all the grisly details retailed to the public by way of pamphlets.

Emerging from the evidence of court records and pamphlets is a confused picture of covens operating in the countryside under the presidency of a man who was called the Devil. Dancing in a ring, nudity, sexual intercourse with the 'Devil' and parodies of Christian ritual were a feature of these meetings. A female leader was often referred to as the Maiden. It was believed that witches flew to their meetings, or Sabbats, on broomsticks with the aid of 'flying ointments'. A likely explanation is that by taking hallucinogens such as 'magic mushrooms', which would have been readily available, they may have gained the impression of flying. Witches could supposedly be identified by marks on their bodies: extra nipples from which they suckled their familiars or areas in which they felt no pain.

The persecution of witches was renewed during the period of the Civil War and the Commonwealth, but by now the campaigns in Britain and Europe were losing their impetus. A more enlightened and intellectual age was dawning and the moral certitudes of the ruling class were being replaced by increasing scepticism. It is difficult to date precisely the last official execution of a witch in England, but it was probably around 1690. The fervour lasted longer in Calvinist Scotland, where a woman was burnt at Dornoch in 1722. An Act of Parliament passed in 1736, in the reign of George II, abolished the harsh penal laws, retaining only light sentences for those pretending to use sorcery for purposes of gain. This demonstrates that the authorities were no longer prepared even to acknowledge that witches had existed in the first place, preferring in future to regard them as fraudsters.

The impression lingers today that witches are essentially evil, old, indulge in obscene rituals and are devil worshippers. William Shakespeare must take some of the blame for this, although as a popular playwright he was only reflecting the prejudices of his audience. Ask a cartoonist today to draw a witch and he or she will sketch a hunchback crone with a beaky wart-spotted nose and pointed hat. Doubtless she will be stirring a brew in a bubbling cauldron, yet that implement was the only form of cooking pot possessed by the poor at the time of the persecutions. An accurate cartoon of an environmentally concerned modern witch would represent her preparing a brew in a pressure cooker in order to save energy, or even using a microwave.

The genius of William Shakespeare enables us to focus on the survival of the second strand of ancient knowledge and its influence on Modern Paganism. Shakespeare could caricature the witch, yet the same

21

pen produced such occult plays as *The Tempest* and *A Midsummer Night's Dream*. Elizabeth, his sovereign, was praised extravagantly and as Gloriana was elevated almost to the status of a Goddess. James I, the great persecutor of witches, enjoyed musical plays based on the allegorical themes of the Greek Gods and Goddesses. These court masques, which were elaborately staged and employed the best musicians of the day, presented a Pagan world of beauty and harmony. At the time all members of the educated classes were aware of the Greek legends, which had been revived in the Renaissance a century before and provided the inspiration for poets, artists and composers.

In classical Greece popular and bawdy religious rites catered for the needs of ordinary people while mystery cults were the preserve of priestly initiates. The aim of the mysteries was to give the initiate a sense of spiritual awareness, the ultimate goal being a mystical union with the divine creative force of which the myriad Gods and Goddesses were only popular manifestations. In the sixth century BC, the philosopher-mathematician Pythagoras, who had travelled both in Egypt and India, provided much of the framework upon which occult knowledge is based. In turn Pythagoras was followed by Plato. The Greek philosophers believed that a spiritual reality lay behind the earthly manifestation of the universe. This presupposed a divine spark which granted individual humans immortality. The philosophers also believed in reincarnation through successive lives until spiritual perfection was achieved.

The Romans took over the mystery cults from the Greeks, added the Egyptian Goddess Isis for good measure and, in the process of developing a state religion, lost much of the underlying spiritual message. New monotheistic religions, the worship of the Sun God

Mithras and the Jewish sect known as Christianity, moved in to fill this gap. Initially Christianity struggled to establish its supremacy over a host of rival beliefs before being adopted as the state religion by the Emperor Constantine.

Christianity had a simple pitch: when the world came to an end, only the Christians, as Children of God, would survive to live in an earthly paradise. Part of the attraction of Christianity was that it was available to everyone. The occult tradition had always appealed to a small minority which was capable of understanding. The neo-Platonist school, the last of the great Greek-inspired philosophical movements, continued to speculate until well into the sixth century upon the nature of man's relationship with the cosmos, but its teachings gradually became dispersed. Another movement was Gnosticism, which in one form or another was to be a thorn in the side of Christianity until the early Middle Ages. Essentially the Gnostics believed in a one supreme, unknown and infinite God totally detached from the world, which he did not create. Gnostics believed the creation was performed by a fallen aspect of this God, called the Demiurge, who had imprisoned man by depriving him of the knowledge of the true divinity. Only by gaining that knowledge could the souls of men ascend again into the celestial light.

Gnosticism in one form or other spawned myriad sects, many of which were ascetics rejecting worldly values as evil. Some even thought sex evil because the act of procreation brought another unfortunate soul into the debased world. The last great flowering of such beliefs was among the Cathars of Southern France who were ruthlessly exterminated by the Church in the thirteenth century.

By the early Middle Ages the so-called ancient knowledge may have been driven underground, the classical libraries largely destroyed and unorthodox philosophical speculation banned, but Christianity could never totally subdue the natural curiosity of man. Texts lost in the West began to resurface at the time of the Crusades and many of the returning warriors brought ideas with them which had been culled from Arabic and Jewish sources. The Knights Templar, a military order founded to defend pilgrims to the Holy Land, became as a result immensely wealthy and their dependencies spread throughout Europe. Phillip IV of France, short of money, cast covetous eyes on the Templar wealth and, with the connivance of the Pope, had the order disbanded in 1307 on charges of heresy. Modern historical research has shown that the inner core of the membership did practise a form of occult religion incorporating aspects of the Egyptian mysteries of Isis.

From the Christian point of view, the Templars were seen as having been corrupted by wicked Eastern influences. After the order's disbandment its knowledge was driven underground. Other strands of Eastern knowledge surfaced during the later Middle Ages, probably via the Jewish and Arab communities in Spain, which have had a strong influence on modern occultism. As the study of such abstruse subjects remained the prerogative of a very small intellectual minority, those individuals largely escaped persecution by being clever enough to camouflage their activities.

The great period of intellectual quickening in the fifteenth century, the Renaissance, stimulated a revival of interest in magic and ancient knowledge. Thinkers began consciously to cast aside the blinkers imposed by the Church and, appalled by its corruption, started to re-examine classical literature. By the sixteenth century, as the framework of the Roman church was riven by the Reformation, there was an explosion of literature on magic and mysticism. This did not have much effect on the lives of ordinary people in Europe, being restricted to a literate elite. While an increasingly embattled church tortured, burnt and hanged witches, Marie de Medici, Queen of France, celebrated a Black Mass, the ultimate in Christian parody. Just as there is good and bad in occultism today, the Renaissance brought forth a bewildering mixture of superstitious nonsense and genuine speculation.

A new strand of knowledge was the study of Alchemy, which has often been regarded as a spurious pseudo-science yet remained popular until the seventeenth century. Like most occult themes, the important parts remained under the surface, available only to those who could decode the symbols. At the same time, ritual magic was discovered and a whole series of *grimoires*, or books of instruction appeared, complete with mystical talismans, circles of power and massed hierarchies of archangels and demons. Probably the most important influence on the future, however, was the spread of interest in the Kabbalah, a byproduct of Jewish mysticism the origins of which are extremely ancient.

The Kabbalah, which is based on a symbol known as the Tree of Life, has long been regarded as the key with which to unlock the corpus of hidden knowledge. The Tree of Life has ten spheres or *sephiroth* arranged in three columns which can be interpreted as a representation of man and the cosmos. This is a complex subject, stretching way beyond the scope of this book and associated with gematria, the science of numbers, in which words can be given a numerical value and thus take on a magical significance. Modern students interpret the major cards of a Tarot pack in terms of Kabbalistic thinking.

The Renaissance inspired artists and writers to take up previously forbidden Pagan themes. Wealthy patrons, often from among the higher clergy, vied with each other to adorn their palaces with images of Gods and Goddesses. The Tudor court in Britain adopted the new artistic fashion while remaining Christian in outlook. At the same time Europe was torn apart by wars of religion, as the forces of the Reformation fought those of the Counter-Reformation.

One effect of the so-called new learning, coupled with revulsion at the activities of the Christian fanatics, was to foment a spirit of scepticism and anti-clericalism in Europe. The eighteenth century has been called the Age of Enlightenment, in which philosophers, freed from the threat of persecution, felt free at last openly to criticize not only Christianity but also the concept of religion. Occultism drifted into the doldrums, although Freemasonry flourished. The Masonic concept of the universal brotherhood of man was in keeping with the spirit of the eighteenth century, and as a secret society it became extremely popular among the middle class. In those days there was a strong occult background to Freemasonry, which today has largely degenerated into purely ceremonial activity without the psychological impetus of magic.

Freemasonry was widespread in eighteenth–century Britain, from whence it spread to America, and was to play an important role in the occult revival during the Victorian era. In addition, the gentry became fascinated by Pagan themes, reflected in the artefacts they acquired during their grand tours of the sites of Greek and Roman antiquity. They filled their Palladian county houses with statues of the classical Gods and Goddesses, while their Christianity subsided into outward conformity. It was only among the lower orders, crammed into the smoking mills of the Industrial Revolution, that non-conformism took hold. To a large extent this sounded the death-knell of the remnants of country Paganism in Britain.

❦ 2 ❦
The Revival

In the eighteenth century, occultism had all but died out, sustained only within the Masonic Lodges. Towards the end of the nineteenth century it experienced a dramatic revival in the hands of a middle class with money and time to spare. The renewed pursuit of occult study did not develop into a mass movement, nor did it take on a religious form. It was driven by sheer curiosity and the revival of interest in the Middle Ages during the Victorian era. The sciences of psychology and psychiatry, which have so greatly influenced the way we see the human mind today, were in their infancy at the turn of the century, which explains the naivety of many supposed adepts of that period.

Pseudo-medievalism has always been popular with European occultists, and in Britain has often adopted exaggerated forms. The Devil was still just around the corner to send shivers through the souls of righteous people and give them a thrill at the same time. Towards the end of the eighteenth century, a group of young degenerates led by Sir Francis Dashwood had founded the notorious Hell Fire Club, based at Medmenham on the Thames. Here they practised a form of dilettante diabolism which gained considerable contemporary notoriety. The theme of the dissolute nobleman selling his soul to the Satan has always been popular with novelists. In 1801, an Englishman, Francis Barret, wrote a book entitled *The Magus or Celestial Intelligencer*, a hotch-potch of scraps from earlier works complete with pictures of the obligatory demons, which claimed to be 'a complete system of occult philosophy'. That it certainly was not.

The most influential writer to bring occultism to a wider public was a Frenchman, Albert-Louis Constant (1810–75), who Judaicised his name to Eliphas Lévy. His work is almost unreadable today, but it does provide a

of modern occultism depends. He also wrote about the Tarot cards and how to interpret them, lifting them from the realm of the gypsy fortune-teller into their rightful place as a symbolic key to knowledge.

By providing a body of knowledge, however hedged about by obscure language, writers took occult wisdom out of the hands of secret societies, who passed on their tradition orally, and for the first time made it available to all. In turn this made it possible for cranks and imposters of all kinds to gull a credulous audience.

Spiritualism provides a good example. The spiritualist movement became popular in the United States in the middle of the nineteenth century and soon spread to Britain. The desire of people to communicate with the spirits of the dead was easily manipulated by fraudulent mediums, and the resulting exposures served only to damage the image of the occult as a whole. Speculation did not play a great part in the Victorian Age, which was dominated by the development of technology, the pursuit of material progress and immense advances in scientific knowledge. Against the latter, the established churches fought a series of bitter rearguard action. Charles Darwin, for example, was castigated for suggesting that we might be descended from monkeys rather than having been created by the direct will of God. Nevertheless, the Victorians possessed a seemingly inexhaustible interest in the past which inspired a new breed of amateur scholars and antiquaries whose research found its way into print. The new railways opened up the countryside to the explorer, making it possible for ancient sites like Stonehenge to be visited by parties of curious gentlefolk. Inevitably, the increased study of the world of antiquity led to the discovery of old magical texts which, while often misunderstood, began to appear in print.

In Britain the most important event in the revival of occultism occurred in 1888 with the formation of the Order of the Golden Dawn. Although the Order's membership never exceeded one hundred, its practices and rituals have since become the framework for ritual magicians in this country.

The story of the Order began when two doctors, W.R. Woodman and William Wyn Westcott, claimed to have found some old papers detailing magical rituals and containing the address of a mysterious German woman, Anna Sprengel, who subsequently authenticated them. In fact, Anna Sprengel never existed and the manuscript may well have been a forgery. The two Englishmen were members of a Rosicrucian order called the *Societas Rosicruciana in Anglia*, which then existed on the fringes of Masonry. Rosicrucianism originated in Germany in the early seventeenth century and its philosophy was essentially Gnostic, proclaiming the need for the soul to rise above the temptations of the world.

An early recruit to the Golden Dawn and its driving force was Samuel Liddell Mathers, who took the name MacGregor Mathers, sometimes styled himself Comte de Glenstrae and liked to dress up in Highland costume. Undoubtedly Mathers was a fraud, but he translated a number of ancient manuscripts in the the British Museum and the library of the Arsenal in Paris, as well as founding the Isis-Urania Lodge in London. Drawing on Egyptian, neo-Platonist, Rosicrucian, Kabbalistic and Masonic sources, among many, Mathers produced a vast and complex system of rituals, which have since been published in full by Israel Regardie. As in Masonic practice, a number of degrees or grades governed admission and advancement within the Order and were conferred in initiatory rituals.

hierarchy of supposed higher adepts to confer advancement and, inevitably, quarrels broke out as to who was to be in charge. Eventually the Order broke up with various members departing to found their own organizations. The Irish poet W.B. Yeats was a prominent member at one time, as was A.E. Waite, who wrote a number of books on magic and devised the most popular pack of Tarot cards still in use today. Partly responsible for the break-up was an extremely unruly member, the young Aleister Crowley, the self-styled Master Therion, the Great Beast 666 of the *Book of Revelations*.

Crowley is interesting in so far as he exerted, and still exerts, a considerable influence on occult thought in Britain. He has been reviled by many while others hail him as the greatest magician of the twentieth century. The truth lies somewhere in between. Crowley was an exceedingly unpleasant man, devious, callous towards women, bisexual, a heroin addict and self-publicist. Yet he was capable of writing poetry of great beauty, and his vast output of literature on magic will stand the test of time. Most of his works were privately published during his lifetime, but have subsequently been reissued to reach a wider public. It is a paradox that occult wisdom has so often been made available though disreputable channels, and the difference between the charlatan and the true sage is frequently difficult to discern.

Crowley was born in 1875 and on reaching his majority inherited a considerable fortune. His early upbringing was amidst the strict confines of the Plymouth Brethren which perhaps explains his later excesses. As a young man he travelled widely, was an expert mountaineer and immersed himself in the study of magic. He quarrelled with the Golden Dawn because its leaders would not promote him through the grades as rapidly as he wished. He took his revenge by founding his own order, the Astrum Argentum. At one stage he set himself up with his followers in a mansion in Scotland, and later moved to Cefalu in Sicily. Controversy dogged him during his lifetime and he died in 1947 in the obscurity of a boarding house in Hastings.

Another spurious but influential nineteenth-century occult movement was the Theosophical Society, founded in 1875 by Madame Helena Blavatsky. David Conway wrote of her: 'Madame Blavatsky's life, far from blameless, is one which those hostile to esoteric matters always retell with great relish. Unfortunately, their hostility blinds them to the fact that what Mme Blavatsky had to *say* is a thousand times more valuable than anything this charming old fraud — if indeed, such she was — ever *did*.'

Madame Blavatsky certainly had considerable psychic powers and spent much of her life tirelessly travelling around the East, where she claimed to have received tuition from mysterious Tibetan adepts. Although accused of forgery and the faking of psychic manifestations, she presided over a society which at its height had more than 100,000 members worldwide. It flourishes today, as does one of its offshoots, the Anthroposophic movement founded by Rudolf Steiner.

The serious study of the more esoteric forms of the occult which began at the end of the nineteenth century was carried over into the twentieth. Crowley resurfaced in England after the First World War, but by then was a spent force. Hounded by the press, he sank into oblivion. During the same period, Violet Firth, who came from the Golden Dawn tradition and used the pen name Dion Fortune, wrote a series of books on magic, both fictional and factual, which are still immensely readable today. She also founded the Fraternity of the Inner Light which unsuccessfully endeavoured to combine Paganism and Christian mysticism.

By the 1930s such subjects as ceremonial magic, Eastern mysticism, Tarot and Kabbalah had been explored. Other factors were also at work in society at large which were to encourage the rebirth of the old witch cult. There was a reawakening of interest in folklore and country matters. This was principally a pastime of the urban middle class, but it also reflected a popular reaction against city life. Its origins lay in the Arts and Crafts movement at the turn of the century. With the advent of mass transport, the countryside became readily accessible to townspeople. People became interested in folk songs and legends. Rambling clubs flourished, youth hostels were established and there was an attempt to recapture the spirit of a rural golden age which, in truth, had never existed.

A new and related academic discipline was anthropology. Fraser's famous work, *The Golden Bough*, which dealt in depth with primitive religion, was first published in 1922. Crucial to the reawakening of interests in witch-craft, however, were the works of the well-known Egyptologist Margaret Murray. In 1921 she published *The Witch Cult in Western Europe*, and this was followed in 1933 by *The God of the Witches*. Miss Murray claimed that witchcraft was a survival of the old fertility-based religion and deduced from the evidence of the witch trials of the seventeenth century that there had been a cohesive organisation into covens. This is now regarded as an exaggerated picture, but her research formed a valid basis for speculation. She also claimed that the old ideas of a sacrificial victim king had survived and cited William Rufus and Thomas à Becket as examples. More important, though, were the references her books made to the worship of a Goddess resembling the Greek Diana, a mother figure and consort of the Horned God. Previously scant attention had been paid to the female role in fertility – seventeenth-century inquisitors were more interested in evidence of the Devil. Margaret Murray may well have paved the way towards restoring the Goddess to her rightful place in peoples' consciousness.

In 1951 the remaining statutes against Witchcraft were repealed and replaced by legislation dealing with fraudulent mediums. Many writers on Witchcraft have hailed this as a momentous event which enabled them to step out of the closet. But the original laws passed in 1735 imposed penalties only on those who claimed to use witch power for false gain. The last prosecution under the 1735 law was of a spiritualist medium in 1944 who was accused of 'pretending' to go into a trance. The repeal of the act was the excuse for Gerald Brosseau Gardner to reveal some of the secrets of the Craft in his book *Witchcraft Today*, published in 1954.

Gardner was born in Lancashire in 1884 into a prosperous family, and subsequently went off to the Far East where be became a tea and rubber planter in Malaya. He then joined the Customs service there and retired in 1936, taking up residence in Bournemouth. He married the daughter of a parson in 1927 and they lived happily together although she never shared his interests in witchcraft. During his time in the East, Gardner, although not formally educated, contributed a number of articles about local customs to learned journals and wrote a book about Malay ceremonial daggers. At that time he did not appear to have any interest in occultism, but when he returned to England he took up naturism and became a co-Mason, a branch of Freemasonry which admits women on equal terms. He also knew the then head of the Druid order.

Gardner claimed that he had been initiated into a traditional witch coven in the New Forest in September 1939. The coven was run by a woman called Dorothy Clutterbuck and it was from her group that Gardner claimed to have learned the secrets which had survived the times of persecution. Several of Gardner's detractors were convinced that this was pure invention, but research by Doreen Valiente has proved that Dorothy Clutterbuck was a real person. She was a member of an amateur theatre group based in Christchurch which called itself The Rosicrucian Fellowship of Crotona, which Gardner joined shortly before the war.

What the coven actually did and who the members were is unknown, although they apparently worked a ritual to stop Hitler from invading Britain in 1940. Gardner told Doreen Valiente that they danced in a circle chanting to form their spell. As the invasion never materialized, they could probably claim that it worked! Certainly there was no written liturgy on which their rituals were based and thus their ceremonies would have been fairly simple ones, without the trappings that have since crept into the Craft. Also unknown is the pre-history of the coven. As Dorothy Clutterbuck came from a well-to-do family and belonged to a Rosicrucian theatre group, the coven could well have been formed by middle-class romanticists who had read their Margaret Murray and enjoyed dancing about in the nude. On the other hand, it could have been a genuine survival from a much older tradition handed down through the generations by word of mouth.

In 1949 Gardner wrote a novel entitled *High Magic's Aid* which was published by Michael Houghton, the proprietor of an occult bookshop near the British Museum in London. The author was named on the cover as Scire, which was Gardner's witch name. It did not sell well and Gardner may well have financed the publication himself. In the novel he described the initiation of a witch, which involved nudity. It is unclear when he formed his own coven, but Doreen Valiente was initiated by him in 1953 in a house in Christchurch owned by a woman member. The coven usually met in Gardner's flat in London or at a hut near St Albans which he had erected on land adjacent to a naturist club to which he belonged and from which several of his witches came.

Many present-day followers of Gardnerian witchcraft choose to legitimize their beliefs and practices by avowing that Gardner's cult owed its origins to the teachings of the New Forest coven. In the immediate post-war period, however, he was influenced by other occult strands which have nothing to do with native witchcraft. At some time between 1945, when Aleister Crowley moved to Hastings, and his death there in

December 1947, Gardner visited the ageing 'Great Beast', having been introduced to him by the late Arnold Crowther. The two men subsequently met on several occasions and Crowley made Gardner a member of his occult society, the O.T.O. (Ordo Templo Orientalis), complete with a parchment scroll and impressive wax seal. The O.T.O., which had German origins, was much concerned with sex magic, and had borrowed much from Freemasonry, including a complicated system of degrees. Doreen Valiente dismisses the order by saying that it was virtually defunct at the time and initiation consisted of being given the rituals to read.

There is evidence, however, that Gardner was heavily involved in the O.T.O. Kenneth Grant, who became Crowley's literary executor and took over the leadership of the order from him, wrote an interesting commentary on the works of the esoteric artist Austin Osman Spare (1886–1956), who was also an accomplished magician. That book, *Images and Oracles of Austin Osman Spare*, published in 1975, was dedicated to the late Michael Houghton, the bookshop proprietor who had published Gardner's novel. Grant states that he introduced Gardner to Spare and that they both played a part in the New Isis Lodge, a branch of the O.T.O. Spare was involved both in performing and illustrating specific sexual rituals, and provided clients, one of whom was Gerald Gardner, with talismans incorporating the symbols of that branch of esoteric magic.

Grant writes that in 1955 he met a woman named Clanda 'who had but recently belonged to a coven of witches formed by Gerald Gardner'. Apparently she failed to find fulfilment in her role as priestess there and had joined the New Isis Lodge. Gardner took exception to this and wrote to an occult magazine criticizing the members of the New Isis Lodge. He then asked Spare to make him a talisman for 'restoring stolen property to its rightful place', the property in question being Clanda. Behaviour of this kind is out of keeping with the strong moral and magical ethics required of members of the Gardnerian cult. Another connection is made by Doreen Valiente who says that Grant was present at a ritual held by Gardner in 1949 which involved circumambulating a large sigil that had been painted by Spare.

By the early 1950s Gardner, who mixed in Masonic circles and was involved both in a naturist club and a lodge of ceremonial magicians using the power of sex, had formed a witch coven which met regularly. As a basis for their rituals he wrote a series of texts which he called the *Book of Shadows*, principally culled from known sources. Gardner borrowed much of its language from Freemasonry and imported large chunks wholesale from Crowley and the old *grimoires* of the ceremonial magicians. Much of the texts' philosophy came from Margaret Murray. Doreen Valiente, who disliked the emphasis on Crowley, rewrote sections of the original collection and added some beautiful poetry of her own. The entire work has been published by Janet and Stewart Farrar together with an analysis of the various versions, and it is clear that the *Book of Shadows* contains little material which came from the New Forest coven. Nevertheless, the *Book of Shadows* material has given great spiritual contentment to many thousands of people who have since worked the rituals.

In 1954 Gardner published *Witchcraft Today*, tricking it out with spurious academic language and footnotes. In the book Gardner claims that he has been 'permitted' by the witches to write of certain things but that others must remain eternally secret. Naturally he does not reveal who gave him permission but he leaves the impression that he was acting as spokesman for the witches of Britain. The book sold well and was published two years later as a paperback. By then Gardner had established himself at Castletown in the Isle of Man as the director of The Museum of Magic and Witchcraft.

Gardner was genuinely convinced that he had a mission to re-create the old Pagan religion of Britain and make it available to the general public. However, the many interviews he naively gave the popular press were distorted into a campaign against black magic and devil worship. Foolishly, Gardner also claimed academic qualifications he did not possess, believing that he would not be taken seriously unless he had the status of a Doctor of Philosophy and Master of Arts.

Gardner's love is publicity led to a split in the original coven. One group, led by Doreen Valiente preferred to work in secret and felt that newspaper articles were counterproductive. She said: 'He could not seem to see the absurdity of initiating people and swearing them to secrecy and then having them read the next weekend some silly interview he had given to the Sunday papers'. In spite of his many faults, however, Gerald Gardner sowed a seed that has since borne fruit throughout Britain and in many other countries. He has had his detractors. His interest in ritual flagellation, nudity, bondage and sex made it easy to depict him as the archetypal dirty old man, but those who knew him loved him in spite of their frequent exasperation at his antics. Many of those he initiated went on to form their own covens and to spread the knowledge he had given them. They were proud to call themselves Gardnerian witches.

Gardner's new religion, which he called Wicca, caught the tide of new thinking which flowed through the 1960s. There was far more to the sixties than Flower

Power and cannabis-smoking hippies. Young people also embraced the peace and civil rights movements and there was a growing ecological awareness. Witchcraft also benefited directly from the increasing concern about women's rights, which were suppressed by the mainstream religions. Conventional Christianity seemed to be in decline and many sought a different form of personal spiritual fulfilment. Sects proliferated and the Beatles joined the pilgrimage to the East in search of enlightenment. The spread of interest in witchcraft and Paganism as a form of alternative religion was one of many manifestations of the spiritual hunger of the time.

During the 1960s Wicca spread slowly but steadily. Like all religious movements, it suffered from factionalism. Gardner's *Book of Shadows* had established a framework, but this did not prevent witches claiming that their own ideas were more 'authentic'. The covens of that period, however, kept a low profile, as the members were painfully aware of the effects of the adverse publicity created by Gardner's urge to hog the limelight. Few witches were prepared to 'come out', and recruitment tended to be by word of mouth and personal contact. Internal feuding found an outlet in the columns of small duplicated newsletters and magazines. There were fewer inhibitions in the United States, land of infinite religious possibilities, where witchcraft was adapted and endlessly readapted. Covens were also formed in Australia and in northern European countries, drawing on the Gardnerian material as the original source of inspiration.

Another controversial figure played a significant role in the revival of witchcraft. The early life of the late Alex Sanders is still shrouded in mystery although one source states that he was born in 1926. For many years he claimed that he had been initiated by his Welsh grandmother when he was seven, but the truth is rather more prosaic. He was initiated in 1961 by a woman who had been a member of a coven in Sheffield and had started up on her own. The original Sheffield group was run by Patricia and Arnold Crowther who were followers of Gerald Gardner. Shortly before the latter died, Sanders visited him in the Isle of Man. During that visit he was permitted to copy Gardner's *Book of Shadows*.

Like Gardner, Sanders had a desperate need to impress people. In his early years he set the development of Wicca back by his publicity-seeking escapades. In 1962 he claimed to be the leader of a coven which conducted rituals at Alderley Edge, near Manchester, and permitted a journalist to take pictures. Overnight Sanders became a regular 'rentawitch' in the tabloid newspapers. This outraged the Gardnerian witches, who accused him of being an upstart and a mountebank. There was more than a little truth in such criticism, particularly as the elements of his rituals which were published had been taken in their entirety from the original *Book of Shadows*.

In 1965 Sanders married a young woman of 18, Maxine, in a Wiccan ceremony on Alderley Edge. Unbeknown to the bride, he had invited the press. The following morning she was revealed to readers in her nakedness, questioned by the police and thrown out by her landlady. Two years later the couple married legally and moved to London where they ran a successful coven in Notting Hill and Sanders assumed the title King of the Witches. All serious witches emphasise that their beliefs are non-hierarchichal and that there has never been a King of the Witches, or for that matter a Queen. Sanders also adopted a spurious Greek knighthood and even attempted to demonstrate magical rituals in a cabaret act. In 1973 Alex and Maxine separated, partly as a result of his openly acknowledged bisexuality, and he went into semi-retirement in Bexhill on the South Coast, where he died in 1988. His funeral was an occult ceremony.

There was much of the charlatan about Sanders, but he possessed genuine ability and many have testified to his clairvoyant and healing powers. The publicity he generated certainly brought the Old Religion to a wider audience, but the damage he did has taken a long time to heal. The Gardnerian witches denied the legitimacy of the initiations Sanders carried out and thus a sect of 'Alexandrians' was formed. Most Gardnerian covens insist that a new member who has already been initiated as an Alexandrian be re-initiated into their own tradition although there is relatively little difference between the two. Vivienne Crowley aptly defines the Alexandrians as 'High Church' and the Gardnerians as 'Low Church', an allusion to the more theatrical taste in ritual preferred by the Alexandrians.

Subsequently, other versions of Wicca have emerged. An American, Raymond Buckland, devised Seax Wicca, which draws on Nordic and Saxon God forms rather than the Celtic sources of Gerald Gardner. The published rituals are simpler and Buckland claims that the Saxon witches' *Book of Shadows* was written down for the first time during the persecutions so that the material would not become lost. However, a separate Nordic strand of witchcraft never existed in Britain and Buckland's rituals follow the basic Wiccan pattern. Buckland's principal innovation was to introduce the principle of self-dedication, which enabled his followers to practice Seax Wicca without having to learn the secrets from an established coven. The modern Pagan scene in Britain has been enriched by followers of various Nordic paths with which many people of English ethnic origin feel more affinity than Celtic mysticism.

Another import from the United States is Dianic or feminist Wicca which caters for women's need to express their spiritual aspirations without undue male interference. Some Dianic covens exclude men while others admit the more enlightened type of male. Many cults in the ancient world were based around a group of priestesses. Although Gardner's coven had a High Priestess, he was a male authoritarian, as have been many of his successors. It is only in comparatively recent times that Wicca has assumed a much stronger feminine orientation, taking its cue from the feminist movement. In some respects the witchcraft and feminist movements have developed hand in hand. Witchcraft revealed a spiritual path which enabled women to take their rightful place at the altar as priestesses in both mixed groups and with other women, and this has helped the spread of Paganism.

The largest cohesive grouping within the Pagan revival in Britain — the 'reinvention' of the witch cult — is represented by the various forms of the Wiccan religion inspired by Gerald Gardner. It is difficult to estimate the numbers of adherents because of the secrecy with which many covens and individuals still surround themselves. During the 1960s and early 1970s Britain's witches could be counted in hundreds rather than thousands. It was not until the late seventies that Wicca began a rapid expansion stimulated by a series of books which set out rituals and enabled people to initiate themselves and form their own covens. Many witches disapproved of publication of their 'secrets', and the writers who did so were castigated in the columns of Wiccan newsletters. However, had the Craft continued to perpetuate itself in exclusive covens, it would have become fossilized. The opening up of the rituals has enriched the lives of many people and their input has provided a valuable cross-fertilization.

For many people, Stonehenge is synonymous with the Druids performing their robed ceremony to celebrate the Summer Solstice. Many of the modern Druid groups are Pagan, but like Wicca they are a re-creation, owing little to the original bearers of the name, about whom the available knowledge is sparse. Other Druid organizations are concerned with such matters as Celtic culture and language, which are compatible with Christianity. Paradoxically, Druids in Britain have never attracted the adverse publicity directed at the witches. The popular conception seems to be that Druids are harmless if slightly dotty people, like Morris Dancers and other folklore groups. Whenever Wiccan groups have attempted to hold publicized ceremonies, they have been hounded by the press and the local Christians alleging devil worship.

The original Druids were the priests and teachers of the Celtic peoples. They conducted their rituals in sacred groves rather than using the older stone circles. Both Roman and subsequent Christian persecution nearly wiped them out, but a few may have survived, living an underground existence. In Wales and Ireland much Druidic wisdom was retained in the stories and legends which, in spite of a Christian overlay, continued to be told throughout the Middle Ages, keeping the old languages alive. There is no evidence, however, of a Druidic priesthood remaining intact even in the most remote corners of the Celtic lands. Like the witches, Druidry faded away through lack of a written tradition.

Interest in Druidry seems to have resurfaced at the end of the seventeenth century when John Aubrey, a noted antiquarian, examined the monuments at Avebury and Stonehenge. He correctly stated that they were much older than the Roman occupation but incorrectly associated them with the Druids. It is claimed by some modern groups that the Order was founded in 1717 at a meeting in a London tavern, but there is no evidence to support this. Whatever the truth, there are a number of Druid orders today, most of which have been founded comparatively recently. Like the Wiccans, they celebrate the eight great festivals of the ancient Celtic year, but do not work magically. They are more concerned with self-development and environmental matters, than the more esoteric aspects of witchraft.

Shamanism, another Pagan strand with a contemporary appeal has its origins in distant tribal times when the witch doctor, or shaman, formed an early type of priesthood by using intuition rather than complicated ritual to divine the future and to perform magic. Drumming and chanting feature in many modern shamanic practices as a means of inducing the altered state of consciousness in which knowledge may be gained. North American Indian practices are popular as well as ideas gained from Nordic legends about the warrior path and a strong belief in the power of totem animals. Shamanism is difficult to define as it is often the preoccupation of individuals and appears in many forms.

Witchcraft and adherence to the various Druid groups involved a membership of a group and adherence to its rules. During the Pagan revival numerous magical orders or lodges appeared and disappeared, although not all of them were Pagan in character. Shamanism, for example, can be seen as an alternative for those, mainly young, people who were interested in Paganism but did not want to be 'initiated' into a group. The notion of structure was anathema to them. In its widest sense Paganism is an attitude to life which may or may not express itself in active worship. In recent years Paganism as a nature religion has drawn strength from the environmental movement and has been spread by New Age travellers and peace campaigners. New Age literature now reaches a wide public interested in such diverse subjects as ley lines, ancient sites, alternative medicine and the occult.

This phenomenon owes much to to the explosion of youth culture in the early 1960s. The open-air rock festival became one of the symbols of the youth movement. Their influence ran far beyond the music which hundreds of thousands flocked to hear. Young people camped, shared their food and talked about peace and love.

The larger the festivals became the more they exhibited a naked commercialism at odds with the aspirations of their audience. In 1970 Jimi Hendrix played on the Isle of Wight to a crowd estimated at 200,000. Outside the festival perimeter, those who could not afford to get in organized their own event and were entertained by a band of young musicians who called themselves Hawkwind. In the same year, Michael Eavis, the owner of Worthy Farm near Glastonbury threw open his fields for the first time and the famous pyramid stage was erected. The inaugural Glastonbury Fayre was described by the music journalist Mick Farran, as: 'a community sharing possessions, living with the environment, maintaining their culture with whatever is naturally available, consuming their needs and little else. It was a powerful vision.'

The early 1970s also saw the establishment of an annual free festival in Windsor Great Park which was inspired by communes of London-based squatters under the slogan, 'Pay no Rent'. These phenomena did much to encourage the adoption of Pagan ideas.

In 1973 Phil Russell decided to reclaim Stonehenge for the people and make it a place of annual pilgrimage. He claimed that Stonehenge's original deed of gift provided for universal free access, a right now denied by cordoning off the monument. In 1974 Russell, who had adopted the name of Wally Hope, printed thousands of leaflets and a group camped for nine weeks in a field near the stones. Ridiculed in the press as the 'Wallies' and battered by the elements, they nevertheless had a good time and were largely left in peace by the police. Wally himself was arrested in 1975 for possession of a minute quantity of the drug LSD and ended up in a mental hospital where drug therapy reduced him to a cabbage. He missed the festival and in September committed suicide. Many festivalgoers still believe that the government had conspired to eliminate the 'leader of the hippies'.

The annual Stonehenge free festival continued through the 1970s. The attendances steadily increased, in a spirit of genuine co-operation between the National Trust who owned the land, the Department of the Environment, which was responsible for the monument itself, the tenant farmer and the police. A blind eye was turned to the fact that, in theory, the event was illegal. A growing sense of environmental concern grew from these events, which some would ascribe to the magic of Stonehenge itself. Sid Rawle, one of the founding fathers of the free festival became a respected figure at Stonehenge and started naming children within the circle of stones. The hippies co-existed happily with the Druids, who conducted their ceremony at sunrise on the day of the Summer Solstice, introducing a spiritual element to what had begun as a protest and Rock festival. At the Solstice weekend each year, the hard core of festivalgoers was swollen by large numbers of town dwellers eager to enjoy the carnival atmosphere and recharge their spiritual batteries.

In the early 1980s new trends became apparent within the free festival movement, which was now losing its fragile cohesion. Disaffected town dwellers, alienated from urban society, took to the roads in old buses, vans and trucks. In 1982 a convoy of 250 vehicles left Stonehenge to travel to the US cruise missile base at Greenham Common to support the women's peace camp there. This marked the beginning of what became known as the 'Peace Convoy', many of whose members were involved with the Ecology Party. That year, on Michael Eavis' land near Glastonbury, the first Green Gathering led to the establishment of the Green collective. 'We have always been a Glastonbury collective. From the start we wanted to link in with the Glastonbury legends and help awaken the spirit of Avalon. I don't believe that anyone could label the spirit that flows through the gatherings and the Collective, but it's very strong. . . At the 1983 gathering we carved a totem pole in the middle of the largest tipi circle ever seen outside North America.'

The 1984 gathering at Stonehenge was the largest and destined to be the last. Of the estimated 30,000 people who camped on the site, only a minority were Green or New Age travellers. The majority had been attracted by the carnival atmosphere, the bands and easy availability of drugs, which was a recipe for trouble. The authorities gave notice that they would ban the 1985 festival. The police, who had gained valuable experience during the miners' strike, were prepared. The Pagan, anarchic ethos of the festival movement had no place in the Britain of Mrs Thatcher. The Green element of the Convoy ended in 1984 by establishing the Rainbow Fields Village at RAF Molesworth, the site of the second cruise missile base in Britain. Some 150 men, women and children overwintered there, living in an assortment of vehicles, tipis and tents. On 5 February 1985 they were evicted by riot police, encouraged by Michael Heseltine the Minister of the Environment, who dressed for the occasion in a combat jacket. Bruce Garrard, who was involved with the Green Collective from its inception, wrote about a conversation he had at Molesworth, which indicates how the Rainbow people saw themselves at the time. 'We were talking about our people, about our culture, about our tribe; about Glastonbury as the lap of the Mother and about Stonehenge out on Salisbury Plain in the open, exposed to the wind, as a place to gather together to claim our power, for ourselves, for each other, for the tribe; for the Rainbow Tribe that was finding itself and its name up there at Rainbow Fields.'

The new Pagan spirit forged in the free festival movement had little in common with semi-detached witchery, and its followers had scant time for dogma and the trappings of ceremonial magic. Photographs of the gatherings of the period show bands of bedraggled but happy people, many of them going naked. The movement was infused by a strong feminist element of the gentler sort, and much of its spiritual ethos was borrowed from the shamanism of the North American Indians. If any deity was worshipped, it was the Earth as Mother, coupled with a desire to recapture the Pagan Celtic past. There was no priesthood, no initiation ceremonies and no structure. Ritual developed spontaneously with circle-dancing, chanting, drumming and the use of mantras. The only bond was a sense of belonging to a very special tribe and a genuine desire to love, to share and to care for the Earth Spirit.

After the break-up of Rainbow Fields Village, the community it housed went their separate ways. A group of tribespeople based in Glastonbury founded the Free State of Avalonia; others acquired land in Wales and settled there as Tipi Village. Some stayed on the road as travellers; others established themselves as smallholders.

Because of its connections with Arthurian legend, Glastonbury has always been popular with the mystically inclined. Before the war, Dion Fortune lived there. Today the small Somerset town is a centre of pilgrimage for New Age types of many different persuasions, and a thriving tourist industry has developed to cater for their needs. Glastonbury High Street is a kaleidoscope of vegetarian cafés, shops selling occult bric-à-brac, booksellers, art galleries and therapists. Parked beside the kerb among the modern cars, the visitor may spot a pony and cart or a colourfully painted van. The local inhabitants have mixed feelings about the newcomers but realize that the town thrives during the season, whether they like it or not. The Free State of Avalonia, a term coined for Glastonbury by many of its New Age residents, co-exists uneasily but on the whole peacefully with the Christian Glastonbury based around the Abbey ruins and living off the legend of Joseph of Aramathea.

In this beautiful part of the world Paganism survives as a living entity.

❧ 3 ❧
The Ethics of Witchcraft and the Realities of Magic

All religions have an ethical or moral framework which has either been laid down by a
hierarchy, revealed in some sacred book or has
evolved though custom and practice. The mainstream
patriarchal religions have tended to hedge in their
followers with 'do nots' which have taken on the status
of taboos, and all display a preoccupation with sin in one
form or another. The taboos themselves are often
dietary, such as a prohibition on eating pork or insisting
on fish on Friday. Others concern sexuality. The basis of
the revealed religions — Islam, Judaism and Christianity
— is the repression of their followers. Independent
thought, particularly in theocratic states, often prompts
persecution. The *fatwah* issued against the novelist
Salman Rushdie, author of *The Satanic Verses*, illustrates
the very narrow range of tolerance permitted in a state
where Islamic fundamentalists hold sway.

Nevertheless, when stripped of its more lunatic
encrustations the religious impulse at the level of the

individual prompts broadly similar patterns of behaviour among the devout followers of organized religions. There are many Christians, Muslims and Jews who lead lives of service to their fellow human beings, are careful not to consume more of the Earth's resources than they need, and treat those who happen to think differently with tolerance. In this sense Pagan beliefs, which may seem strange to those who are confronted by them for the first time, are not fundamentally at variance with those held by other religions.

Modern Pagans subscribe to a single law which regulates their approach both to their own lives and the lives of others; 'Do as thou wilt, and it harm none.' This formula was devised by Gerald Gardner for his Wiccan followers and has since been adopted by the Pagans of various persuasions. It does not absolve Pagans from observing the basic rules which, in Christian society, for example, derive from the core of the Ten Commandments: respect for one's parents, not killing or stealing. These provide the framework for living in harmony with others.

Gardner borrowed the words of his formula in part from Aleister Crowley, who in turn lifted them from Rabelais. Yet Crowley always stated that his Law of Thelema was revealed to him magically at Cairo in 1904, inspiring his *Book of the Law*. His formulation, which in keeping with most things about Crowley has been always misunderstood, was as follows. 'Do as thou wilt shall be the whole of the Law. Love is the Law, Love under Will.'

These words have been misinterpreted as a licence for all kinds of unprincipled behaviour with no regard for the consequences. In turn this has stoked the evil reputation of the Great Beast 666, as Crowley liked to style himself. But this is to render him a great disservice.

He intended that people should search within themselves for their true will and then accomplish it. In this
way they would discover that their true wills were in
harmony with Nature and the cosmic realities. Crowley
attributed crime to most people's ignorance of their true
will — unification of mind and body with the creative
source. This was by no means a novel approach, as self-
knowledge was the key to the ancient mystery religions
and can equally apply to so many Indian and Oriental
meditational systems. Even the Christian mystic seeks
union with God through prayer and meditation.

The most important characteristic of witch law is
that it places the moral initiative in the hands of each
individual rather than laying down explicit directives.
Every person can exercise his or her right to do as they
please — provided it does not do harm or infringe the
rights of another. Thus you can play music late at night if
you want to, but not if the noise will disturb the neighbours' sleep. All those who live by this simple law must
think for themselves at all times and apply it to each and
every activity. In sexual morality, for instance, there is no
prohibition *per se* of adultery. But, anyone who wishes to
embark on such an extra-marital affair must consider the
likely effects on their own partner and children as well as
on the partner and family of their lover. Nothing in life is
ever quite as simple as it sounds.

What happens to the witch or Pagan who breaks the
law? In worldly terms, nothing. They are not branded as
sinners from the pulpit or excommunicated with due
ceremony. There is no ritual of confession, penance and
the doling out of a set number of repetitive Hail Marys
and Our Fathers, after which one can, in theory at least,
commit the same offence again. The concepts of Heaven
and Hell do not exist for Pagans, hence their anger when
they are branded as Devil worshippers. One can only

worship the Devil if you believe in both him and the reality of the realm over which he is presumed to preside. Instead, Pagans accept the reality of reincarnation, another ancient belief, and the concept of *karma*, which is an import from the East.

In Pagan terms the concepts of reincarnation and *karma* are interlinked. Pagans believe that we all have a number of lives or incarnations on this earth. Human lives are seen as a progression through which it is hoped that the soul will learn lessons, improve itself and ultimately reach a level of awareness of cosmic reality, an awareness of the ultimate purpose of creation, after which there will be no more need to reincarnate. At that stage the soul begins its ascent on to the higher levels of non-physical existence on the astral plane. This explains the terms sometimes used to describe people as being young souls or old souls. The former are either at the start of the process or have somehow become stuck, concerned purely with material pleasures and the satisfaction of bodily desires, taking no interest in anything that does not directly concern their own gratification. Old souls, on the other hand, are those more enlightened individuals who think of others before themselves, become involved in the caring professions, are concerned about environmental issues and question their own position in the tapestry of existence. At the end of the chain of incarnations are the 'saints', known in Sanskrit as the *bodhisattvas*, who can voluntarily choose to return once more in order to teach.

The second concept, the Law of *Karma*, has been likened to a spiritual bank balance which we accumulate during successive incarnations. By exerting our freedom of will, we can either squander or work to increase it. Essentially it can be expressed in terms of cause and effect: 'what ye sow, so shall ye reap'.

Everything that a person does in life, whether good or bad, sets up waves around himself or herself, like the ripples caused by throwing a stone into a pond. Eventually those ripples will flow back in accordance with the law of balance within the universe. Every action has an equal and opposite reaction. Every evil deed must be rebalanced by a good one somewhere down the line if harmony is to be maintained. All this underlies the basic Pagan law, as one has to live with any harm done and come to terms with it.

Karma has nothing to do with punishment. There is no angel writing down one's misdeeds in a heavenly ledger that will be held against one at the moment of death. *Karma* is impersonal and as immutable as the universe itself. It applies to everyone, whether or not they believe in it. Under *Karmic* Law, an evil life may be followed by a series of incarnations to restore the *karmic* equilibrium. We all possess a conscience, in that instinctively we know when we have done something wrong. Some are able to ignore the dictates of that inner voice and may even be tempted to think that they can get away with it. Those who follow the dictates of their conscience, however, realize when they have stepped out of line and will do their best to remedy the damage they have caused, whether to themselves or others. Thus the *karmic* debt can be repaid swiftly. If one observes the careers of totally evil people who somehow seem 'to get away with it', the temptation is to feel that there is no justice. But their *karmic* debt will have to be repaid, and one can argue that the very presence of evil in the world is there to teach us opposite values.

Pagans can have no idea what will happen to them when they die and what the process of reincarnation will be. The general belief among Pagans is in the concept of a period of rest after death followed by conscious preparation for physical rebirth. The Celts saw the afterworld, which they called The Summerlands, as a reality and not a place of dread to be feared. The souls of the dead embarked from the western shore and sailed away towards the setting sun where they could take their ease before returning. One common view is that the place we will go to when we die will express what each of us might wish for. Perhaps the passionate golfer will find himself on the perfect course with a never-ending supply of balls. From the many accounts of people who have had near-death experiences it is clear that when the spirit leaves the body there is a sense of great peace and a vision of beauty.

Because of their belief in reincarnation and the workings of *Karmic* Law, Pagans have no fear of death, which makes life itself far less complicated. However, although Pagans might build their lives around the principle of harming no one, not all Pagans are necessarily 'good'. There are those who claim to ascribe to Pagan ethics but still behave in anti-social ways. Moreover, as there is no book of rules to follow, what is good for one may be bad for another.

Where, perhaps, Paganism differs from the mainstream religions is in the emphasis placed on individual responsibility at a moral level. Each must accept responsibility for his or her actions at all times. There can be no reliance on others for definitions of right and wrong. In the Pagan world there are no gurus who can promise painless solutions to everyone's problems. The majority of Pagan folk that I have encountered, love life unashamedly and are well-balanced, tolerant and generous, not only to their own kind but also to all their fellow humans. They are angered by intolerance, violence, greed, cruelty, oppression of the rights of the individual, bigotry and the despoiling of the planet.

The subject of magic can lead to much misunderstanding and moral confusion. Magic is integral to the belief system of witches but is not actively worked by all Pagans. The best definition of magic was coined by Aleister Crowley as 'the art of causing changes in conformity with the will of the magician'. The operative word is *change*, and anyone can cause change by the use of willpower.

Almost everyone seems to be fascinated by the word magic. People often refer, for example to 'the magic of childhood'. Children, their minds uncluttered by adult values, can accept magic as a fact of life without questioning the premises on which it is based. Yet magic is not a Pagan prerogative and can equally well be practised by people of any religious persuasion. After all, Roman Catholics believe that in the mass the priest, through consecration, causes the bread and wine to become the actual flesh and blood of Jesus.

In its various guises magic remains a neutral force, the effect of which depends on the intention of those working it. There is white or right-hand magic where the aim is to achieve a good result; and black or left-hand working which aims to achieve the opposite. In between there are various shades of grey magic where the moral parameters can easily become blurred. Any magician can work either white or black magic as the techniques employed are identical—only the intention differs. This follows the Law of Polarity, which sees everything in the universe as having a complementary opposite — night and day, male and female, right and left, black and white etc. It is the application of that polarity that can either be destructive or constructive, not the principle itself. A witch who works magic and is bound by the basic Pagan Law *can* work black magic but would not contemplate it. There are those who work black magic, most of whom are foolish sensation seekers. They are not Pagans and are shunned by witch covens.

Magic is governed by the Law of Three-fold Return, which states that the results of any magical activity will rebound on the magician with triple force. If someone consciously sets out to harm someone else magically, there will be a boomerang effect with greatly increased force. In contrast those who consciously work with love for others will receive love in return, and their lives will be consequently enriched. In addition there are a number of other forces which have a bearing on the result of a magical working or spell. A practitioner of magic ritual cannot cause an amputated limb to regrow, but he or she can use magic to help the patient's body to cope with the after-effects of such a loss. A further factor that influences the outcome of magical activity is the cause and effect nature of *karma*. For example, healing magic will not work on an illness which lies within the patient's *karmic* pattern. Spells which frequently do not work include those for gaining money or material possessions, for obtaining influence over others, moral or intellectual blackmail and revenge. Perhaps this explains why there seem to be few rich witches around!

Witches have told me, and writers on magic have confirmed, that they are most frequently asked to perform attraction magic, or love spells, an activity which involves many moral dilemmas and prohibitions. The bringing of two people together by exerting your will over theirs may impose a *karmic* responsibility which could rebound unpleasantly on the magician. A magician with the necessary skills can attract a partner of the opposite sex but might find himself or herself bound in mutual loathing to that person for all eternity. Another cause of failure can be traced to the wills of the persons for whom the magic is designed. Vivienne Crowley cites a typical case: 'Sometimes we may have worked very hard to help someone to sell their house, only for completion of the sale to be continually thwarted by a whole series of extremely unlikely mischances. Here witches have to be good psychologists and try to find the source of the "blockage". Is the person secretly afraid of change and unwilling to leave the familiarity of their old town? Is it perhaps their partner who is unwilling; do they want different things?'

Timing is also important. It is said that astrological influences can have a bearing on the best time to work a particular spell, but the most important factor is the phase of the moon. When the moon is waxing it has a positive influence which increases as it reaches its fullness, the reason why covens traditionally meet on the night of the full moon. During a waxing moon, spells can be worked which are designed to have a positive outcome. During a waning moon, on the other hand, only spells designed to eliminate negative aspects will be successful. This will have nothing to do with black magic unless the practitioner so wills it. White witches, however, can work 'banishing rituals' such as ridding someone's house of a bad atmosphere or dispelling the negative effects of an illness. All genuine witches condemn attempts to do direct harm to someone, but can work to hinder harm being done. For example, a case of child abuse might be brought to the notice of a coven. *Karmic* law makes it impossible to curse the perpetrators or visit them with some terrible affliction, but it would be permissible to work towards blocking them from continuing their evil activities.

Magic not only has a strong moral foundation but its working goes hand in hand with the broad sweep of Pagan ethics. Marian Green states that 'the purpose of magic is to help each individual become the most effective, competent and skilled person he or she is capable of being.' In other words, the individual must sort himself or herself out before embarking on magical activity. As magic is an intellectual operation that requires lengthy psychic training, it follows that the practitioner's mind must be in good trim before starting to explore the subject.

Magic can be practised in many ways, all of which can be equally valid given the circumstances of the group or individual concerned. Its principal subdivision is into high and low magic. The former represents the traditional intellectual magic developed through the centuries by the mystics and the secret orders and involving complicated ritual, magnificent robes and much equipment. Low magic is that practised by the traditional village healer. It is the magic of nature and of the elements and its practitioners often rely more on intuition than intellect. Gerald Gardner plundered the world of the ceremonial magicians and used many of their ritual ideas as well as creating his own imagined and idealized picture of the witches of the past. The magic worked in Wicca, while tending more towards the low variety, can also display many of the trappings of high magic.

In practical terms a second subdivision can be made between the magic worked in a coven or group and that worked by an individual or partnership who may or may not also be members of a coven. David Conway, a noted ceremonial magician, has likened the working of magic to an equilateral triangle, the three sides of which he has labelled intention, imagination and concentration. If any one of the three elements is missing, the desired effect will not be achieved. The magician must have a clear picture of the desired result of his work and no doubts about its ethical implications. He must then imagine that result happening and concentrate his entire will into bringing it about. You can experience the process at work should you find yourself at the theatre sitting behind a woman wearing a large hat which hides the stage. Your intention is quite clear; that she should remove it. You need then to be able to imagine her doing so by visualizing her actions in your mind and to concentrate on it happening. It works!

These three elements are the nuts and bolts of making magic, and the methods used depend largely on individual preference as to ritual trappings. Equipment and method are only the triggers that activate the psyche and prompt the practitioner who has not fully developed the skills of visualization.

In Wiccan covens, although much depends on the ability and particular interests of the high priestess, much of the magic worked is for healing purposes. There are workings aimed at the solving of the problems of individual members of the coven or those of their friends: the selling of a house, for example, or success in an examination. On a wider level, magic might be worked in the cause of world peace or a healthier environment.

In a coven or group, witches are principally concerned with low magic and refer to their activities as 'raising power', usually by means of dancing in a circle and chanting a repetitive refrain. The intention will have been discussed beforehand and agreement reached on the visualization of what everyone wants to happen. There are, perhaps, parallels to be found here in the chanting of Christian evangelical congregations, with their 'Hallelujahs' and cries of 'Praise the Lord'. It is no chance that a popular modern hymn is entitled 'The Lord of the Dance'. Dancing in a circle and chanting goes way back into the mists of time and is common to all forms of primitive religion in which the shaman led the tribe in a dance, imitating the actions of the animals they desired to hunt. A persistent feature of the evidence in the seventeenth-century witch trials is the confession by the defendants that they danced in a circle. The chant used today can consist of meaningless words, such as 'Eko, Eko, Azarack', or one specifically written with the intention in mind. The healing rune used by many witches is:

> This is the spell that we intone
> Flesh to flesh and bone to bone
> Sinew to sinew and vein to vein
> And each one shall be whole again.

The first purpose of the dance is to merge the individuality of the participants into the group mind or soul. By the linking of hands and a surrender to the flow of words and movement, a strong bond is forged by the group. One only has to think of thousands of Welsh rugby fans singing 'Guide me O thou Great Jehovah' at Cardiff Arms Park to appreciate how much power can be raised by such communal action. It is no wonder that the Puritans frowned so much on the ecstatic delight of dancing, which in many of the ancient religions was a prelude to a bout of group fertility, notably in the worship of Dionysus in Greece. Secondly, the dance releases etheric energy from the participants which forms the so-called 'cone of power'. It is the task of the priestess leading the ritual to bind the energy raised and to direct it into the ether as a powerful thought form.

Another magic 'trigger' popular both with groups and individuals is the use of a candle as the basis of a spell. The colour of the candle is important as the magical textbooks give lists of correspondences which are often at variance with each another. The generally accepted ones are as follows:

White: Peace, spirituality, purity.

Red: Health, energy, sexual potency, strength.

Pink: Love, romance.

Yellow: Intellect, memory, creative mental work.

Green: Luck, fertility, abundance.

Blue: Protection, intuition, spiritual knowledge.

Orange: Career, law.

Let us imagine that you wish to help a friend who is ill. Choose a new red candle and then take some pure natural oil and 'dress' the candle by rubbing the oil into it, starting from the top and working towards the middle and then upwards from the bottom. While doing this, think about your friend and what it is that you would like for him or her. When the candle is ready, take a match and light it. As the flame burns, sit in front of it and imagine your friend, lying in the hospital bed. Try to visualize the scene as strongly as you can — even smell the antiseptic. Then, when you can hold the scene steady, visualize the light of the candle diffusing in a warm glow around the patient and then imagine him or her as you would like them to be: walking in a field, perhaps, or sitting happily in the pub. Chant a short rhyme. For example,

> Candle candle burning bright
> In the darkness of the night
> Give (name) the strength to fight
> And come back to the light.

Finish by saying quite firmly: 'This is my will, so shall it be.' Leave the candle to burn out, ensuring that it does not drip or fall over. This is a simple spell, based on different versions quoted in books as well as recommended by individual witches I have known. Anyone can work this magic without courting danger, and if one accepts the underlying premise of magic. It will work if the person carrying it out really wants it to. It is not even exclusively Pagan; a Christian could perform such a ritual, dedicating it to the will of Jesus.

With a little imagination, a candle spell can be adapted to many circumstances: cleansing a room in a house or flat, for example, or passing an examination. Low magic can also be used to charge an amulet or talisman. Most of us have had such an object at one time or another: a lucky Saint Christopher in the car, a favourite Teddy Bear, a mascot tucked away in pocket or handbag, a golfer's 'lucky' pullover. The keeping of these objects of personal reverence answers a deep and universal human need. The *grimoires* of the ceremonial magicians gave hugely complicated instructions, full of angelic names of power and fragments of Hebrew, for the charging of talismans. In terms of low magic, however, anything will suffice. Using the appropriate consecration ritual, anyone can turn a simple stone into a talisman for their own or their friend's personal protection. Choose a small pebble, or piece of crystal, that feels right for the purpose you have in mind. Wash it carefully and carry it around with you for a while so that it takes on your own aura. Then, if the purpose is to banish bad influences, choose a night of a waning moon and consecrate it with water, salt, incense and a candle flame, firmly stating the intention.

The fashioning of a wax image or doll, an ancient example of sympathetic magic often used by witches, is sometimes misinterpreted as a form of black working. As the only difference between white and black is one of intention, it follows that the use of such an image is perfectly legitimate for those who follow the right-hand path. The aim is to make a small doll that represents the person for whom the working is being undertaken and to personalize it, if possible, with a few strands of hair or some nail clippings from the subject. The doll is then consecrated and given the name of the person it represents, after which those carrying out the work handle it in turn, addressing it by name and willing the intention into it. At the end of the working it is wrapped in a cloth whose colour corresponds to the intention and is hidden away where it cannot be touched. When the spell has either worked or failed, the doll is broken into small pieces which are thrown into a stream of running water with a commendation for it to return to the elements from which it came.

Like everything else in Paganism, there are no hard and fast rules to be applied to someone who wishes to work magic. There are those who have a natural affinity for magic and already possess psychic or clairvoyant ability. Others who choose the Pagan path have a more cerebral approach and need to map the area carefully with reading and practical experiment. The vital ingredient on which all are agreed is the need to develop through meditation, the powers of visualization. Mind power is the key to all magic. Some Pagans also take up yoga or gentle martial arts disciplines like tai chi which simultaneously train body and mind.

Magic is also active in divination. Divination has been bound up with human nature right from the earliest times when the tribal shaman used omens such as the flight of birds to determine the weather or the right time to plant a crop. Prophetic oracles were enormously popular in ancient Greece, and in Rome the priesthood studied the entrails of sacrificed animals to work out the auguries for the outcome of military campaigns.

Janet and Stewart Farrar have defined divination as 'clairvoyance with tools' in which the 'tool' used acts as a trigger for the subconscious intuitive side of our natures which often lies buried under layers of precon-ditioning. A number of different methods are used today of which the Tarot cards are the most popular. Tarot cards appeared during the late Middle Ages although it is probable that they are much older. In parts of Europe there are packs of playing cards known as Tarot, but they have little or nothing to do with the divinatory cards that are on sale in such bewildering variety today. A Tarot pack consists of four suits of the so-called Minor Arcana; Wands, Swords, Pentacles and Cups, running from ace to king. Instead of the usual knave, there is a page and a knight. There are fifty-six cards in all, each with a different picture. In addition there are the Major Arcana, twenty-two cards each representing an arche-type, such as the Magician, the Fool, the Hermit, the Wheel of Fortune and Temperance.

The skilled Tarot reader sets out the cards in a certain pattern and, by looking at them, sinks into a form of light trance in which the images on the pictures trigger a response in the psyche, leading to an interpretation. Some witches read Tarot professionally, but the over-whelming majority will not take money for their services. Similar tools of divination are the Chinese I Ching and the Nordic Rune stones. Again, the quality of the divination depends on ability of the practitioner and not with the tool itself.

Also within the field of divination are such methods as scrying and dowsing. The former is traditionally practised by looking into a crystal ball and analysing the images that form as the seeker enters the trance state. Good quality pure rock crystal balls are now very expensive and often beyond the pocket of the local witch. An inexpensive substitute can be made by painting the inside of a bowl matt black and filling it with water; some use a concave mirror with a black background. The scrying tool acts as a focus for the release of the subconscious and has no intrinsic worth within itself.

The traditional country dowser looks for water using a forked hazel twig which will vibrate in the hands over a source. Another method is to take two pieces of coathanger wire and bend them into an L shape. Slide the two shorter ends into lengths of plastic tube which you hold in your hands so that the wires can swing freely. If you walk over a water main or underground stream, the two free ends will cross. It is essential to empty your mind while dowsing, concentrate on an image of water.

Another dowsing device, the pendulum, was extensively investigated over a number of years by an archaeologist T.C. Lethbridge. The pendulum consists of a small weight (a piece of crystal, a small stone or a button) suspended from a length of thin twine or cord. Lethbridge discovered that all substances give off a certain vibration or 'ray' and that by altering the length of the cord the dowser can tune out any other objects. The cord length for silver, for example, is given as twenty-two inches, so if you wish to locate a silver item you have lost, adjust your pendulum to that length and move it over the area of search, holding the cord between thumb and forefinger. When it is over the object it will start to rotate quite strongly.

The author Colin Wilson, who has made an extensive study of the occult, devotes a section of his book *Mysteries* to the work of Lethbridge. He suggests the following experiment. Take a suitable pendulum and hold it in turn over the inside of each wrist with a cord length of around nine inches. Over the left wrist it will swing in an anti-clockwise direction and, over the right, in a clockwise direction. There is no satisfactory explanation for this phenomenon.

The speed and angle of swing may vary from individual to individual from an ellipse to a direct left-to-right or circular movement. A clockwise movement is generally seen as having masculine attributes, while an anti-clockwise motion denotes the female side. Thus, in theory, you can sex an unborn child in the womb by holding the pendulum over the belly of the mother. An increasing number of healers are turning to the pendulum as an aid to diagnosis. By passing it over the body of their patient, they can observe the swings and locate the seat of the ailment. It can also be used to answer questions, but only those in which the questioner has no vested interest in the answer, as there is always the danger of auto-suggestion in these circumstances.

Witchcraft and Paganism have a highly developed sense of ethical responsibility, and for witches the practice of magic is an integral part of their structure of belief. In the simple examples I have provided — which are open for anyone to try — nobody conjures up the 'devil' or desecrates Christian or other religious symbols. Those who work magic are convinced that their own and many other lives are enriched by their beliefs.

Many enemies of magic point to the dangers of 'dabbling in the occult'. It is true that magic can be just as dangerous as walking off the kerb without looking out for the traffic. Tuning into the psyche can open up realms of infinite possibility for expanding the mind, but if that mind has not first been strengthened by positive

thought, unpleasant layers buried deep within can surface to cause distress. Those who advocate the practice
of magic always insist that the would-be practitioners
must first take the trouble to get to know themselves. If
the intention is pure, the gods will look after those who
restrict themselves to low or natural magic. Those who
walk in love and humility with the gods will be well
cared for.

❦ 4 ❦
The Pagan Deities

For those who have been brought up within the
confines of a monotheistic religion, the bewildering variety of Pagan gods and goddesses, can
be extremely confusing. God, the omnipotent and all-
seeing male divinity who rules in heaven, tolerates no
competition, even from those who call him Allah or
Jehovah. Modern Pagans often refer to the 'Old Gods',
and the purpose of this chapter is to examine the nature
of the deities they worship. They may well be 'old' but
they never went away; rather, they went underground.
Even the most fanatical Christian is aware of them,
knows their names and many of their attributes, yet will
still regard them as superstitions. Eighteenth-century
noblemen delighted in filling their gardens with statues
of the Greek deities, complete with fig leaves or discreetly draped wisps of cloth, yet still attended the
parish church every Sunday. In Europe powerful
prelates were patrons of the arts, decorating their
palaces with Pagan imagery and commissioning music

which celebrated the rites of the classical deities.

The concept of 'god' is extremely difficult to define. In everyday life expressions such as 'for God's sake' or 'thank God' trip easily from the tongue and the majority of people are quite prepared to accept the reality of 'somebody up there' who happens to be a man. This factor divides the Pagan world from the beliefs of the mainstream patriarchal religions, Islam, Judaism and Christianity. (Hindus are pantheists and have much in common with Pagans in Britain.)

Pagans acknowledge the reality of an ultimate creative force but regard it as impersonal and infinite. They believe that everything created must contain an element of that force. Thus, every human being is a god, endowed with the divine spark. Every plant, tree, animal, insect or fish has that same spark; sensitive people can feel the presence of elemental spirits, or *devas*, in natural springs, caves, rock formations and all other manifestations of Nature. Most Pagans would accept the Gaia theory which posits that the entire planet is a living entity. In other words, the world we inhabit was not 'created' by God but is God itself. In the story told in the Book of Genesis, God granted 'dominion' over the animal and vegetable kingdoms to mankind, which perhaps explains the seeming indifference to environmental issues displayed by many of the Christian churches. It certainly explains why Paganism, in its several forms, is the natural religion of the Green movement.

The origins of the Pagan deities opens up the question of the polarity of male and female. Early human beings instinctively understood this phenomenon through the process of mating and procreation. They realised that their very existence depended on the interaction between a male and a female. Armed with this knowledge, it was logical to assume that the force behind the vital natural resources needed for survival must be of both sexes. The earliest deities were identified as the mother goddess and father god, and in the course of time were endowed with human attributes and took on human forms. As sex was the key to human reproduction, the god and goddess ruled over fertility and their mystical mating ensured the regular changing of the seasons. A further intuitive step was to identify the goddess with the moon/night and the god with the sun/day, each dependent on one another but as separate parts of the whole, the creative force or Nature itself.

A primitive tribe's instinctive understanding was rationalized in course of time as intellectual ability developed. Over several thousand years the Egyptians created a pantheon of Gods and Goddesses, ascribing to them responsibilities for various aspects of life both in the physical world and in the world after death. They were numerous but they all represented aspects of the essential divine polarity. The Egyptians also understood that behind this array of deities lay a supreme creative force, which they called Amoun, the 'hidden one'. As time passed, the Greeks, the Romans, the Indians, the Celts, the North Americans and the South Americans all developed broadly similar pantheons. Although the emphasis differed, the mythical basis remained the polarity between a goddess and a god. The Greeks and Romans readily assimilated and worshipped the Egyptian Isis, and many Pagans today accept her as the original and paramount Mother Goddess.

The ancient Pagan world of nature deities, unashamed fecundity and tolerance of such 'unnatural' practices as homosexuality was anathema to pious Jews. That small section of the polyglot Middle Eastern world had developed into a male-oriented society which imposed a rigid code of sexual morals. Jewish men viewed nakedness in the Greek bath houses with horror. 'Thou shalt not bow down to graven images' was naturally applied to the figure of the Goddess in her naked ebullient beauty clad only in a necklace of acorns. As Judaism was restricted to members of a certain race and did not actively seek converts, it was never a serious challenge in the world of classical antiquity. Christianity, however, although initially persecuted by the Romans, confronted the Mediterranean world head on with its own particular form of Judaism. It did so at a time when Paganism in Rome had ossified into a formal state religion which had lost the vital spark of spirituality.

Today many Pagans invoke a supposed Golden Age of antiquity peopled with classical or Egyptian gods and goddesses. But far more constructive thought has been devoted to the nature of divinity itself. Some Pagans see their gods and goddesses as being purely imaginary entities and products of the group mind. Others believe that they are real, although existing on a higher plane. By personifying them, human beings can more easily enter into a relationship with them. The thoughts and writings of Carl Jung have done much to define the modern Pagan approach to divinity. Jung emphasized that every human being has an unconscious contra-sexual side, the *animus* or male and *anima* or female, which are both essential components of the soul and with which we have to come to terms. Accepting the gentle, intuitive, caring side of his nature — the *anima* within — is often very difficult for a man, preconditioned as he is by society to project a 'macho' image. A woman, too, must learn to accept the male aspect of her own inner nature. Wiccan worship's strength lies in the stressing of polarity. When men and women fuse

their minds together in a circle, they gain an understanding of each other's psychic entity.

Another concept explored by Jung laid down a theory
of archetypes, defined as 'figurative symbols present in
the collective unconscious of all humanity'. We are all
familiar with simple archetypes such as Mother, Father,
Child. As the reality of the divine is quite beyond our
human understanding, we create archetypes which
attempt to reveal a glimpse of the truth. Christian archetypes are God as a solemn bearded man; Mary, young
and beautiful in a blue robe; Jesus, in robe and sandals
surrounded by children; and the Devil complete with
horns, tail and red tights. Pagans use a different set of
archetypes to represent the same basic human requirement, calling them gods and goddesses: Herne, the stag
lord of the forest; Diana, the virgin huntress; Aphrodite,
the love goddess; Mercury, the messenger with his
winged feet; and Merlin, the wise man. Fantasy tales are
full of these archetypes, which exert a powerful effect
on the psyche of the reader. The same applies to the
symbolic pictures in a pack of Tarot cards. A further point
is that a thought form which may have originated as
something purely imaginary, becomes endowed with
power through centuries of worship and ritual, entering
into the group mind of a race or tribe.

In their rituals Wiccans place a far greater emphasis on
the goddess than on the god. This is in keeping with
their philosophy and links them directly to ancient
times. Even Christians could not ignore the feminine
aspect, although they downgraded the archetype,
clothed her decently and desexualised her as Mary the
Virgin. Nevertheless, there have been many paintings,
especially during the Renaissance period, which showed
a highly erotic image of Mary as the Mother, bare
breasted and scantily draped. The role played by the

Goddess in Wicca also helps to explain why women find it so attractive. Banned for centuries from exercising their natural right to priesthood, women have discovered that Wicca enables them to realise the Goddess within themselves.

The occult writer Dion Fortune stated that all the gods are one god and all the goddesses are one goddess. Over the centuries she has had many names: Diana, Isis, Astarte, Rhiannon, Cerridwen, Freya, Hecate, Ceres, Dana. The list is seemingly endless. Each goddess has her legends and her worshippers, but at base each remains an aspect of the primordial Earth Mother — she who was, is and always will be. All versions of the goddess stem from her, have been endowed with different forms and have their own individual attributes.

In keeping with the universal principle of polarity, the goddess is seen as having a bright or positive side to her nature and a dark or negative side. It is the latter which has always aroused fear in men, with its undertones of evil female archetypes — the hag-like witches in Macbeth or the wicked stepmother of countless fairy tales. Yet every thinking man who has loved a woman knows her light and dark moments and her cycle as seductress, comforter and inspirer. Pagans who have mastered fear of the unknown see the dark side of their Goddess as a positive aspect in that she represents the world of dreams, intuition and the inner invisible light. She is seen as the Dark Mother we meet at death, but she is also a friend who leads us back into the light of rebirth and the knowledge of her other aspect, the Bright Mother.

The goddess has also traditionally been regarded as a trinity, far older than father, son and holy spirit. Her three aspects are maid, mother and crone, reflecting both the cycle of life and the waxing, full and waning

Moon. At springtime there is the virgin, almost childlike maiden who mates with the God. In summer she is the mother, pregnant and fruitful. As autumn turns into winter she becomes the old woman, the guardian of the portals of the Underworld. This is reflected in the ritual pattern of the Pagan year, which is described in a later chapter.

Pagans see the goddess as a reality rather than an abstraction, and she exists in all her different aspects within each one of us. She is the key to the understanding of our inner psyche and to the women's mysteries, the Moon and the menstrual cycle. Gerald Gardner called her Aradia, a name which he borrowed from Leland's book, *Aradia: The Gospel of the Witches*, which was published around the turn of the century. Leland had met a woman from Florence who claimed that she was an hereditary witch. According to her, Aradia was the daughter of Diana and her brother/lover, Lucifer. The latter literally means bringer of light and, as far as Pagans are concerned, has nothing whatsoever to do with Satan. Those Wiccan covens which adhere to Gardner's *Book of Shadows*, as well as many others, worship Aradia as their principal goddess. Those who follow the Nordic path refer to her as Freya while the more Celtic-oriented groups use names such as Cerridwen, Arianrhod or Rhiannon. Feminist witchcraft prefers Diana, the prototype of many goddesses, while many Pagans who are not committed to any 'system' of worship are quite happy with a more abstract Great Mother figure.

The Goddess, however, cannot exist without the God, and again we encounter a new series of archetypes around which countless legends have been woven. As the consort of the goddess the Pagan god can be her son and her lover. The goddess is symbolized by the cup, the cauldron, the receptacle; the god by the sword, the spear, the erect penis. 'As the sword is to the male so is the cup to the female, and conjoined they bring blessedness,' is said by a Wiccan priestess when she consecrates the wine in the cup. Many of the tribal creation myths state that the goddess came first and, as the archetypal mother, was the progenitor of the tribe. She gave birth to a son, who grew up and became her lover. That was the only way of explaining things until the advent of the concept of a non-sexual Creator who produced both a man and a woman.

Pagan gods came in a number of archetypal forms, and it is probable that the earliest was the Horned God, who in a hunter-gatherer culture assumed many of the properties of the animals needed for survival. It was natural to give him some of the characteristics of powerful animals, such as the stag or the bull, and as he took on the fertility aspect he became half-man and half-animal, endowed with the lower parts of the concupiscent goat. It was the Horned God, the Forest Lord, who mated with the goddess in Spring, fertilizing the land and its inhabitants. Pan, protector of shepherds and woods in ancient Arcadia, gradually became one of the most important god figures in the Mediterranean, celebrated for his singleminded pursuit of nymphs. Eighteenth-century painters portrayed an ideal pastoral world in which Pan sat on a rock playing his pipes surrounded by adoring and flimsily clad young shepherdesses. In his Celtic guise as Herne or Cernunnos, the horned god is worshipped by Wiccans as a nature deity who has taken on responsibility for environmental problems.

Pan, as a nature and vegetation god, was popular among country folk who were not attracted by the lofty Olympian deities of the towns. He summoned his worshippers into the woods to dance naked, to feast and drink in his honour. Yet he could also inspire the ultimate in terror and it is from this that we derive our word panic. He is not a god to be trifled with or invoked in vain; if awakened, his power can unleash all sorts of misfortunes on unwise magicians. In his Roman guise he was known as Faunus, and to the early Christians his fondness for merrymaking was anathema. His symbolic aspect of cloven hoofs, tail and horns was taken to symbolize the Devil. By depriving the country folk of the protection of the horned god archetype, and the fun which his worship afforded, the Christians condemned millions throughout the centuries to a drab existence.

Another god is associated with the sun in its fertilizing aspect and thus, by transference, mating with a moon goddess to give night and day and the seasons. As patriarchal ideas took hold in Greece and Rome, however, the emphasis on the maleness of the sun caused such gods to be elevated into supreme positions, and some even became identified with the person of the earthly emperor. The list of god forms also included craftsmen gods who forged mythical weapons, underworld Gods who presided over the realms of the dead, crop deities, warlike gods such as Mars and hundreds of small local deities who are today among the most approachable. Our ancestors appointed gods to look after wells, areas of forest, caves and springs. They are the archetypes of figures such as Puck or Robin Goodfellow, and the world of the 'Little People'. Pagans regard it as quite natural when they visit a source of water — a well, for example — to imagine a small, mischievous figure peeping out at them from behind the bushes and honour him with a word of thanks. The old country folk knew and respected such Nature spirits, leaving an offering of food at night.

The old gods are a reality in the daily lives of Pagans.

A favourite toast when gathered with friends is: 'The Old Ones. Merry meet, merry part and merry meet again.' Pagans also say prayers, although in a less formal way than Christians. They like to talk to their Gods, asking them for help and discussing problems with them, rather than reciting set prayers taken from a book. Just as a Christian can pray to God anywhere, so can a Pagan, who has no need of large buildings or ritual equipment. A Pagan may invoke the aid of a particular god or goddess, such as Mercury or the Egyptian physician God, Thoth, for healing.

In certain circumstances when approaching the Gods, some Pagans use a ritual or magical working to take on the *persona* of a god/goddess. In 'assuming a God form' ceremonial magicians apply visualization and will-power to become the god or goddess. In this technique the members of a lodge use a complicated system of colour correspondences, incenses and robes to build up a form or forms in their group mind which is then physically manifested. A well-trained magician can 'assume the form' if one accepts the nature of inner divinity and the historical aim of the mystery religions to enable the initiate to become a god.

A similar practice is employed in Wicca in the ritual known as Drawing Down the Moon which, if correctly handled, can work very powerful magic. Here the priest draws the presence of the Goddess into the body of the priestess. To achieve this, he must have highly developed powers of visualization and imagination. He may be Fred and she may be Jenny at the outset, standing at the altar either robed or naked. As he kneels before her and speaks the invocation he must see her not as Jenny but as the Goddess, transformed by his will. For her part, she will feel an altered state of consciousness and will take on some part of the archetypal power for the duration of the ritual. The same process applies to that most controversial notion, the naked priestess on the altar, beloved by readers of Dennis Wheatley novels and viewers of semi-pornographic videos. The issue of sex in magic is discussed elsewhere in the book, but the point here is that the priestess is not *on* the altar but rather she *is* the altar as she personifies the Goddess herself. One could argue that the same technique is used by a Roman Catholic priest in the Mass when, by consecration, the wafer and wine are transubstantiated into the actual body and blood of Jesus as God.

At the root of all Pagan belief is the acceptance of the divine polarity and the interaction between male and female. As they worship the ancient deities, which never disappeared from our unconscious minds, Pagans see in them the power of Nature. There is a powerful statement of all that the Goddess means to Wiccans in a ritual address known as the Charge. This is declaimed in turn by the priest and priestess at the beginning of a ritual meeting, as if the Goddess herself was speaking. The wording is not secret, but I give it here for the benefit of readers who are unfamiliar with it. Gerald Gardner originally assembled a version drawn mainly from the work of Alesteir Crowley, but this was subsequently rewritten by Doreen Valiente in the form in which it is known today. It is not restricted to Wiccans and its wording is acceptable to most Pagans. As a statement of belief, it accurately encapsulates the essence of modern Paganism.

Priest:
Listen to the words of the Great Mother; she who of old was also called among men Artemis. Astarte, Athene, Dione, Melusine, Aphrodite, Cerridwen, Dana, Arianrhod, Isis, Bride, and by many other names.

Priestess:
Whenever ye have need of anything, once in a month, and
better it be when the moon is full, then shall ye assemble
in some secret place and adore the spirit of me, who am
Queen of all witches. There shall ye assemble, ye who are
fain to learn all sorcery, yet have not won its deepest
secrets; to these will I teach things that are yet unknown.
And ye shall be free from slavery; and as a sign that ye be
truly free, ye shall be naked in your rites; and ye shall
dance, sing, feast, make music and love, all in my praise.
For mine is the ecstasy of the spirit, and mine also is joy
on earth; for my law is love unto all beings. Keep pure
your highest ideal; strive ever towards it; let naught stop
you or turn you aside. For mine is the secret door which
opens upon the Land of Youth, and mine is the cup of
the wine of life, and the Cauldron of Cerridwen, which is
the Holy Grail of immortality. I am the gracious Goddess,
who gives the gift of joy unto the heart of man. Upon
earth, I give knowledge of the spirit eternal; and beyond
death, I give peace, and freedom, and reunion with those
who have gone before. Nor do I demand sacrifice; for
behold, I am the Mother of all living, and my love is
poured out upon the earth.

Priest:
Hear ye the words of the Star Goddess; she in the dust of
whose feet are the hosts of heaven, and whose body en-
circles the universe.

Priestess:
I who am the beauty of the green earth, and the white
Moon among the stars, and the mystery of the waters, and
the desire of the heart of man, call unto thy soul. Arise,
and come unto me. For I am the soul of Nature, who gives
life to the universe. From me all things proceed, and unto
me all things must return; and before my face, beloved of

84

Gods and men, let thine innermost divine self be enfolded in the rapture of the infinite. Let my worship be within the heart that rejoiceth; for behold, all acts of love and pleasure are my rituals. And therefore let there be beauty and strength, power and compassion, honour and humility, mirth and reverence within you. And thou who thinkest to seek for me, know thy seeking and yearning shall avail thee not unless thou knowest the mystery; that if that which thou seekest thou findest not within thee, thou wilt never find it without thee. For behold, I have been with thee from the beginning; and I am that which is attained at the end of desire.

❦ 5 ❦
Entry into
the Craft

All religions have rites of entry or initiation, usually involving a number of common features, such as ritual purification, a declaration of agreement with a set of principles, anointing, or the wearing of special clothing. Infants are normally dedicated to their parents' religion and, on reaching a certain age, are admitted to the ceremonies on the same basis as adults by way of a rite such as confirmation or Bar Mitzvah. Adults who decide to join a particular religion are generally admitted by way of a ceremonial induction. In Wicca, which sees itself as a mystery religion, entry is gained through an initiatory ritual which confers membership of a particular coven as well as to the wider fraternity. Other Pagan groupings have their own initiatory systems, but it is also possible to be a Pagan without joining a coven.

It is often said that 'witches are born, not made'. Although one cannot confirm it with statistics, the Wiccan religion seems to attract people who have reached a certain level in their spiritual development and find a natural home in the teachings of Wicca. Even as recently as the early 1980s, it was extremely difficult to make contact with covens, or any occult group for that matter, but an increase in the number of books and magazines dealing with this and related subjects has stimulated greater openness. Networking channels can now put enquirers in touch with someone in their own area (see the list of addresses at the end of the book). Vivienne Crowley, author of an important book on Wicca, gives a box number in London and welcomes correspondence. Other covens and groups hold regular open meetings at which anyone is welcome to come along and ask questions. Some covens, however, continue to act in total secrecy and can only be approached by way of personal introduction.

Not everyone desires to join a coven or working group, and some may prefer to follow the path of the solo witch, working alone or with a partner. It used to be a strongly held principle that, 'only a witch can make a witch', but as many influential members of the Craft today started out by initiating themselves, this rule has fallen into abeyance. Some would argue that it is better for a novice to have the support and training of a regular coven, but in many cases this is not possible. A considerable breakthrough was the 1978 publication of Doreen Valiente's *Witchcraft for Tomorrow*. This book gives a simple, well-structured outline of Wiccan practices and a shortened version of the *Book of Shadows*. The author was one of the initiates in the original Gerald Gardner coven and wrote much of the material in his book. She produced a ritual of self-initiation that has probably been worked by many people since her book's publication. Nevertheless, this ritual is essentially a self-dedication, as an initiation presupposes the participation of a priest or priestess to reveal the mysteries.

Other initiation rituals are available, notably one devised by Janet and Stewart Farrar and based upon basic Gardnerian principles. In his book *The Tree*, Raymond Buckland sets out a complete system of worship based on Saxon mythology. Alternatively, the candidate can write his or her own ceremony of self-dedication, reflecting perhaps on particular ideals or aims. This would be appropriate for someone who wants to follow a Pagan path without becoming involved in the ritualistic approach of many Wiccan covens.

Self-dedication rituals have a number of shared features which anyone can adapt. The following is an outline based on Wiccan principles and is designed for a female candidate.

Having made the decision, the candidate prepares a working space, which can be in any room where she will be undisturbed, setting up a small table or chest to act as an altar. On the table there might be a vase of flowers, a candle, a joss stick or incense burner, a goblet of wine and some anointing oil. She must also obtain a suitable robe or, even better, make one herself.

Ideally the ritual will be performed on one of the eight great festivals or on the night of a new or full moon. The candidate undresses and takes a bath which can be scented with herbs or oil. The ritual bath is a time for meditating upon the step which she is about to take. The candidate should then enter her working space entirely naked and kneel silently in front of the altar, absorbing the atmosphere cast by the candlelight and the incense. In the basic ritual the self-dedicate might invoke the particular god or goddess form with whom she feels an affinity and make a solemn declaration of intent. Doreen Valiente gives this beautiful affirmation.

I am unique. There is no one else exactly like me. And yet I am one with the whole of Nature.

I have the right to be what I am. My essential self is divine and beautiful. I have the right also to be better than I am, that the outer manifestation may be more true to the inner reality.

Beloved Pan, and all the other gods who haunt this place, grant me beauty in the inward soul, and may the outward and the inward life be at one.

The candidate then anoints herself as a symbolic gesture of purification, marking herself on the forehead, the chest and the genital area, to signify freedom of the mind, the heart and the body. The ceremony ends with the donning of the robe as a symbol of rebirth in a new guise, and the drinking of the wine as a libation.

Gerald Gardner emphasized that Wicca is an initiatory religion in which the candidate is inducted ritually into the mysteries, in contrast to beliefs such as Christianity or Islam in which the beliefs are revealed by a prophet and set out in a holy book. Gardner had been involved in Freemasonry and ceremonial magic, from which he drew many of his ideas. He was initiated into the New Forest coven in September 1939 — the basis for his claims to legitimacy — and laid down three levels of initiation which he called degrees. Akin to Masonic practice, these also conferred rank within the Craft. The first degree, essentially a first step within a coven, made the candidate a witch and priestess or priest. The second degree, a promotion to High Priest or High Priestess, could be conferred after a suitable interval. A second-degree witch can initiate others to the first or second degrees and can form a separate coven under the supervision of the original one. The third degree confers absolute independence.

As one of the main principles of the Craft is male/female polarity, it was laid down that a man must be initiated by a priestess and vice versa. An exception, however, is that a priestess may initiate her own daughter. Gardner also permitted another departure from his rules, in the case of a couple joining together. In theory only a second-degree witch can carry out an initiation, but in this case he can initiate the female witch and then permit her to perform the ceremony for her partner. No hard and fast age limits were set, but the initiation of minors has no place in the Craft. Covens generally set their own limits and twenty-one is a common age at which candidates can be accepted. There is some evidence that in hereditary Witchcraft some form of sexual bonding is required on entry, but this has never been the case in Wicca.

Ceremonial initiation is not the sole prerogative of Wiccan covens. Some of the Druid orders feature ritual induction as do many of the ceremonial magic orders and lodges. The latter have extremely complicated degree structures through which a candidate must advance after lengthy preparation and study. In less exalted societies, there are echoes of traditional initiation rituals that have been corrupted into horseplay. At my school, new boys were stripped and dumped into a cold bath, after which they had to stand naked on a bed and sing the school song while being pelted with pillows. In Germany, the beginning and end of an apprenticeship is often marked with ritual stripping and humiliation of the candidate, echoing perhaps the practices of the medieval Freemasons and other Craft guilds.

In the ancient world, the initiation ceremonies attached to the mystery religions remained a closely guarded secret reserved for the devotees, and we know relatively little about them. In *The Golden Ass*, Apuleius refers only in the broadest terms to his initiation as a priest of Isis. What remains, however, shows that initiation involved purification, nakedness, the suffering of an ordeal, the taking of an oath and the revelation of some secret knowledge. The last may well have been communicated by means of a mystical drama. Essentially, the ceremony was one of ritual death and rebirth, involving a descent into darkness and then re-emergence into light, reclothing and purification. During the process the candidate became identified with the God or Goddess and was thus transformed. The Roman Catholic and High Anglican versions of Christianity retain an element of myth in that the priest at the altar in the consecration of the bread and wine effects the transubstantiation of the elements into the actual flesh and blood of Christ. In the Roman Church children undergo an initiatory experience when they are robed in white to receive their first communion.

Gerald Gardner described the initiation of a priestess in his novel *High Magic's Aid*. Doreen Valiente states that when she was initiated by Gardner in 1953, the ceremony ran along the same lines with the addition of some material which Gardner had lifted from Aleister Crowley and Leland. One solid piece of evidence about ancient initiation ceremonies is to be found in the series of frescoes in the so-called Villa of the Mysteries at Pompeii. Gardner refers to them at some length in his book *Witchcraft Today* and clearly based his views on entry to the Craft on those scenes. They show a young woman being prepared for the ceremony of initiation into the Orphic mysteries, bathed and covered by a veil. One scene shows her kneeling with her head in the lap of a priestess who has bared her back for the ritual scourging. In another she uncovers a basket to reveal a phallus. The final panel shows the initiate dancing ecstatically naked.

Instant initiation is not a feature of modern covens, and any such practice should be avoided. The covens which publicize their activities and offer instruction to would-be candidates impose a waiting period, often of a year and a day, during which the candidate will attend a series of 'open meetings' or 'outer circles'. If the group is a serious one, the candidate will also receive a course of training in the basic principles of the Craft. This sensible precaution enables the coven to weed out unsuitable candidates. It also gives the candidates an opportunity to get to know the members of the coven and make up their own minds if they really wish to join the group. Inevitably, the quality of instruction depends on the capabilities of those running the coven. There are some covens who permit a serious candidate to attend certain rituals before initiation after undergoing a simple ceremony of personal dedication to the ideals of the group.

The full texts of the Gardnerian initiation ceremonies have been published by Janet and Stewart Farrar in *The Witches' Way*. I will restrict myself to discussing the principles and purposes underlying the rituals, which have often been adapted to the needs of particular covens. In Wicca there is no holy writ laid down on tablets of stone, although the principles remain the same. As Wiccans are only human beings, quarrels have surfaced from time to time about the validity of initiations carried out by certain groups who have been accused of sectarianism. Today the Pagan community has adopted a more broad-minded attitude towards niceties of dogma. Nevertheless, many covens require the re-initiation of anyone seeking admission who has been initiated previously into a different coven. This introduces the newcomer to the group mind of the coven and does not imply that the original ceremony was in any way invalid.

The only criteria for the validity of any initiation ceremony are the serious intent of the participants and the capabilities of the person conducting the ceremony. The initiator acts as a conduit for the outside powers that are channelled into the candidate. If he or she cannot establish contact, the ceremony will be no no more than an interesting ritual experience conferring membership of the club. The true purpose of the Wiccan First Degree is to effect a spiritual awakening in the candidate and to provide a pathway into the group ethos of Wiccan beliefs. It is the starting point of a mystical voyage towards self-discovery and the development of the psyche. As a trained psychologist, Vivienne Crowley has looked far more deeply into the Wiccan ethic than other writers, and she defines the First Degree as a rebirth or regeneration. During this the candidate is made aware of the contra-sexual side of his or her nature, the concept of *animus* and *anima* established by Karl Jung.

What follows is a description of the initiation of a female into a coven by a male High Priest and represents a synthesis of modern practice. It is a ceremony for which the initiate will have spent some time preparing and which will effect important changes in her life. It would be most unusual if she was not nervous as she approached this intimate experience, her first step on a journey into the unknown.

When everything is ready the candidate, or postulant as she is called in the *Book of Shadows* is taken to a separate room and asked to undress and let her hair hang loose. She must remove her jewellery, and any make-up or other false adornment. Now she is naked as

94

the day she was born. The physical act of undressing in the presence of another is to signify preparedness to abandon her personality as expressed in the clothing she would normally wear. Nakedness had a part to play in the ancient mystery initiations; in Wiccan covens that work robed, the candidate always enters the circle naked before being reclothed.

The next stage is a ritual bath to signify the start of the purification process, after which the candidate is blind-folded and bound, to signify the darkness and restriction of death. The hands are tied behind the back with a cord, and then pulled upwards to form a triangle with the loose ends of the cord being knotted in front of the throat. Shorter cords are tied around one knee and to loosely tie the ankles together to form a hobble. Thus restricted, the candidate is left alone for a while in silence while the rest of the coven prepare the space where the ceremony will take place. She will be collected and brought in by one of those present who will guide her hesitant steps to the edge of the circle where she will smell the incense and sense the presence of the others.

The High Priest or Priestess will then stand before her and issue a dramatic challenge, placing the point of a sword or ritual knife against her chest so that it can be felt but not break the skin.

> *O thou who standest on the threshold between the pleasant world of men and the terrible domains of the Lords of the Outer Spaces, hast thou the courage to make the passage? For I say truly, it would be better to rush on my blade and perish rather than make the attempt with fear in thy heart.*

Two passwords are then demanded, these being, 'perfect love and perfect trust'. Originally these were secret but their frequent publication has led to their significance becoming common knowledge. The two concepts are integral to the Wiccan ethos and are the frame of reference which determines relationships between members of the close-knit coven. The initiator then hands his sword to the High Priest and gives the candidate a third password, which is a kiss.

The process of crossing the threshold into the circle differs widely. Some covens lay a broomstick across the entry point; the initiator moves behind the candidate after the kiss and pushes her over the threshold, where she is caught by the High Priestess. In other covens the candidate is physically picked up by two witches and carried over. Whatever method the symbolism remains the same, the struggle of the birth pangs and the emergence into the unknown world of the magic circle.

Once inside the candidate is led by the initator to the four cardinal points while the elemental Guardians of air, fire, water and earth are summoned to witness the ceremony. She is then brought back to the centre of the circle and the Charge (quoted in the previous chapter) is read to her. (Sometimes this is read before entry into the circle.) The term comes from Freemasonry and signifies an instruction in which certain principles are revealed.

The next step is also powerfully symbolic and differentiates Wicca from the mainstream religions. The initiator kneels before the bound and blindfold candidate in an attitude of submission. 'In the Art Magical we are taught to be humble' (*Book of Shadows*), and this implies that there are no rulers and no ruled in the Craft. He then gives her the five-fold kiss which is one of the elements seized on by the detractors of Wicca who regard nudity as sinful. With each sentence the appropriate part of the candidate's body is kissed.

Blessed be thy feet that have brought thee in this way.
Blessed by thy knees that shall kneel at the altar.
Blessed be thy womanhood without which we would not be.
Blessed by thy breasts, the fount of all nourishment.
Blesed be thy lips that shall utter the sacred names.

The Farrars coyly place the kiss on the candidate's womanhood, or manhood for that matter, as being 'just above the pubic hair', but as one witch pointed out to me, if you are going to kiss it, do so, otherwise why bother?

Naturally the reaction of many outsiders is one of shock and horror, yet in Wicca, the human body is regarded as sacred and a Temple in which the Goddess and the God dwell.

The next step is called 'taking the measure', which would seem to have ancient traditional origins and which Gardner probably borrowed from the New Forest coven. Using a length of red twine or wool, the measurement is taken from the candidate's feet to the crown of her head. The twine is then cut and further measurements are taken, using the same piece and tying a knot each time, around the head, the chest and the hips. Further refinements in some covens involve pricking the candidate's finger to stain the measure with a drop of her blood, and the cutting of a lock of her hair. Gardner seems to have imagined that in the old covens the lock was kept in order to bind a new member to keep the secrets by implying the measure could be used magically against her if she revealed the coven's secrets. In the Alexandrian tradition the measure is handed back to the candidate to ensure that there is no misunderstanding, Gardnerian covens may still keep measures.

At this stage of the ceremony the candidate is ready for ritual purification and the taking of the oath. She is helped to kneel and her ankles and knees are bound together with the loose cords. She is then asked if she is ready to undergo the ordeal, a ritual scourging, and be purified. Gardner's detractors have claimed that he had an unhealthy interest in flagellation, which may well be true. The purpose, however, was not and is not to cause pain. The scourge used is a few lengths of thin knotted cord which is applied lightly to signify that to learn you must first suffer. Forty strokes in all are given and Vivienne Crowley has written that candidates often complain that they were not hard enough.

After the scourging comes the administration of the oath which enjoins a vow of secrecy on the candidate and forbids the disclosure of the names and addresses of other coven members. The candidate must also vow to reveal the knowledge of the Craft only to suitable persons who are properly prepared. This is a natural safeguard for the other members of the coven as they may well be employed in situations where occult activity would still be frowned upon. In the Gardnerian tradition the candidate chooses a new name, her Witch name; in other systems this is adopted at a later stage. The name may reflect some aspect of the God or Goddess with whom she feels a particular affinity, or aspirations which she may have on the magical path. One witch I know took her grandmother's name as she was particularly close to her. A candidate who has been brought up in a Pagan household, and who was given a hidden name at dedication, may well decide to continue to use it. It is considered bad form to take a name which is not in accord with one's own personality and those who do often appear ridiculous.

Following the oath, the candidate, who is still tightly bound is helped to her feet and anointed. The symbol for the First Degree is the inverted triangle with the point facing downwards, which signifies water. Three anointings are given, with consecrated oil, wine and kisses, in the following order. The genitals, the right breast, the left breast and the genitals once again. Then comes the high point of the ritual when the bonds are released and the blindfold is removed. She has passed through the symbolic death and has been reborn into the freedom and light of her new existence. She sees the blazing candles on the altar and the naked bodies of her new brothers and sisters who greet her with hugs and kisses. The cord which bound her hands is tied around her waist and hence forward, she will always wear the symbol of her initiation when she enters the circle. In some covens, even if they habitually meet naked, the candidate may be ceremonially dressed in a white robe to symbolize her purity.

She is then handed the working tools of a witch one by one — the sword, the ritual knife, the pentacle, the cup, the scourge, the wand and the cords — and their significance is explained. As a final step she is led around the circle to each quarter in turn and it is announced that she has been duly consecrated as a witch and priestess. She will then have an opportunity to consecrate a new ritual knife or any personal jewellery such as an *ankh* or pentagram to symbolize her adherence. Often a present will be given to her by the initiator, for example a ring or a pendant.

The First Degree initiation is the start of a disciplined learning process, entitling the new witch to participate fully in the work of the coven as it celebrates the full moons and the great festivals. If she is a member of a coven with a skilled High Priestess, she will be taught the rituals, meditation, healing, divination and all the other skills that are part and parcel of living the Pagan life. She will learn to gather herbs and will copy out her own Book of Shadows from her initiator's. These activities make up the outward manifestations of the Craft. Within herself her psyche will undergo a series of transformations as she gathers knowledge and begins to re-evaluate herself and her position in the world.

Some witches never advance beyond the First Degree, remaining happy to participate but having no urge to follow a course of instruction over a long period of time. The Second Degree confers the title of High Priestess or High Priest and implies that the candidate is ready to assume the responsibilities of a potential leader, to carry out initiations and to set up his or her own coven. Again, the period of a year and a day is specified between the First and Second Degrees, although it may take longer until a witch is ready for advancement. There is no entitlement and it is a matter of judgement on the part of the initiator to assess someone's readiness.

The ritual of the Second Degree is centred around a drama acted out by the participants and known as the Legend of the Descent of the Goddess. This is a re-enactment of Persephone's descent into the underworld and her confrontation with the Dread Lord of Death. In psychological terms, the candidate is thus enabled to confront within herself the darker side of her nature and to learn to come to terms with it. Unlike most religions, Wicca sees the dark and light sides of our human natures as existing in harmony rather than in conflict with each other.

The ritual begins with the candidate present while the circle is cast, after which she is blindfolded and bound, as in the First Degree ceremony, and led around to each of the cardinal points in turn. This is followed by a symbolic scourging after the question, 'Art thou willing to suffer to learn?' The oath that the candidate swears 'on her past lives and hopes of future ones to come' is a much stronger one than in the First Degree, implying her increased responsibilities in the future. In the next step the initiator kneels beside the candidate and places one hand on her head and one under her knee. Then, using all his concentration, he wills his power into her, giving her all the experience of the entire initiatory chain. That is strong magic and makes the candidate fully the equal of her initiator.

After a moment of silent meditation, the knees and ankles are untied and the candidate is helped to her feet. In some traditions she is then offered the chalice of wine by her initiator, after which he gives her the five-fold kiss. The anointing follows a different pattern as the symbol of the Second Degree is the pentagram with the point downwards, often imagined by Christians to be the mark of the devil. Its true meaning is that the four elements are in harmony but still dominate the fifth element, spirit. The symbol is anointed on the candidate three times, with oil, wine and kisses, in the following order: genital area, right breast, left hip, right hip, left breast and genital area.

After the anointing the blindfold is removed and the candidate is presented with the working tools as in the First Degree ceremony. This time, however, she symbolically uses each one to emphasize her new status within the Craft. The foregoing is a simplification, and in some traditions the ceremony ends with the candidate symbolically scourging her initiator, making the point that all that you do will be returned three-fold.

If the Legend of the Descent of the Goddess is to be performed, the new High Priestess takes on the role of the young Goddess and her initiator that of the Lord of the Underworld. One of those present will play the part of the Guardian of the Portal while another member of the coven reads the text. This is given in full by Janet and Stewart Farrar and is drawn from Greek mythology. It is similar in outline to what we know of the Eleusinian Mysteries which involved the candidate crossing seven thresholds, at each of which she had to remove an item of attire until she arrived in the temple naked. Each threshold involved the candidate being shown an object, such as an ear of corn, and the final rite may well have included ritual intercourse.

In the Wiccan tradition, the naked candidate dons a transparent veil and some jewellery. Vivienne Crowley specifies the seven veils of the original Greek version which, she avers, may well have originated in Babylonian legend. The Guardian challenges her to take off her garments and jewels and then binds her hands. She is then led before the Lord of the Underworld, who wears a symbolic crown and holds a sword. Overwhelmed by her beauty, he lays at her feet the sword and crown, the symbols of his power, and kisses her feet. She replies by stating that she loves him not and asks why he causes all the things she loves to wither and die.

The God replies that it is age and fate against which he is powerless, but that when men die he gives them rest and peace so that they may return. He exhorts the Goddess to stay with him, but she refuses and must submit to Death's scourge. After that he raises her to her feet and gives her the five-fold kiss of love and trust. Then he takes her necklace from the altar and places it around her neck, after which she returns the crown and sword to him.

The ceremony is full of important symbolism although the final act, the sacred marriage, has not been consummated between the God and Goddess at this stage. The fact of reincarnation, however, has been revealed. The Goddess, in descending into the realm of Death, does not die but overcomes her fear. In doing so, she regains her necklace, the symbol of rebirth, and returns once again to the world above.

The final initiatory stage in Wicca is the Third Degree, in which the sacred marriage between Goddess and God is consummated, the background to which is examined in detail in the chapter on sex in Witchcraft. Ritual intercourse, an essential religious ceremony from the earliest times, remains the most misunderstood aspect of the Pagan view. When he developed his Third Degree ritual, Gerald Gardner was drawing on his knowledge of the old religions in order to complete the circle of knowledge. In the First Degree the candidate learns about herself in relation to the Goddess and in the second she is made aware of the God. To complete the circle of knowledge, the two strands must become united within the candidate in the supreme act of creation.

Gardner specified that the rite could be experienced 'in true' or 'in token'. The former meant that penetration of the woman by the man occurred, but this was always to be performed in private and only between two fully consenting adults. If, as some covens insist, the rite is performed in full, complications can ensue when jealous husbands or wives intervene. In practice, the Third Degree is more often than not conferred on a couple who are already established sexual partners and who are ready to move on to form their own coven. In Vivienne Crowley's coven, for example, the High Priest initiates the female candidate in token and she then goes on to initiate her partner in true. The crucial element here is the ability to set aside the human factor, and this is assumed when a witch is ready for the Third Degree. Those involved take on the roles of God and Goddess and are not just coupling to satisfy a brief excess of lust.

The following is an outline of a female candidate receiving the Third Degree from either her partner or the

High Priest who has conducted her previous initiations. Only other Third Degree witches are permitted to be present. There are a number of versions of the ritual and each coven has its own form of words and actions. In the *Book of Shadows* ritual the candidate who takes on the role of the Goddess is seated on a throne and the priest kneels before her in worship. He invokes the power of the Goddess in her and she is then laid down. Ideally this is on an altar which has been cleared of other ritual items, but in practice it is usually on a blanket or sheet on the floor. The candidate's body is aligned on an east-west axis and she lies in the Goddess position with her arms outstretched and her legs parted. In this way the woman forms the altar with her body and is prepared for the ritual marriage. The man who is performing the role of the God kneels beside her and begins a lengthy declamation, after which he moves to kneel between her thighs. He kisses her body in the pattern of the Third Degree symbol, which is an upward pointing pentagram surmounted by an upward pointing triangle.

> *Altar of mysteries manifold*
> *The sacred circle's secret point*
> *Thus I do sign thee of old*
> *With kisses of my lips anoint*
> *Open for me the secret way*
> *The pathway of intelligence*
> *Between the gates of night and day*
> *Beyond the bounds of time and sense.*
> (D. Valiente).

If the ritual is being given in token, at this stage the couple consecrate the chalice of wine and communion is shared between them and the others present. If the ritual is in true, the others leave the circle at this stage, closing the pathway behind them. Thus the celebrants are alone and prepared to participate in the ultimate mystery. The man is imbued with the spirit of the God, kneeling with his manhood erect between the thighs of the Goddess he adores. Slowly he lowers himself over her, covering her body with his. Her womanhood is the Grail, the eternal cauldron of conception and birth. His penis is the magical sword Excalibur, the giver of the life force, the power of the mighty Sun.

> *Let the light crystallise in our blood,*
> *Fulfilling of us resurrection.*
> *For there is no part of us that is not of the Gods.*

As Sword and Grail unite the mystery of the sacred marriage, the *heiros gamos*, is consummated and the egos are united. God and Goddess have become one and the candidate has been given the final key to the understanding of her own psyche.

When they have finished, the celebrants call the others back into the circle. The candidate is then ceremonially anointed with the Third Degree symbol and is taken to the cardinal points to be introduced to the Guardians. Her journey through initiation into the Wiccan tradition has ended and all that remains is to feast and make merry that night.

When executed by a sensitive teacher, this initiatory system is a powerful psychic tool with which to equip a new seeker. The systems used may differ in detail, but they all meet a deep human need. As she develops her knowledge of magic and the Craft, the candidate may undergo other initiations, for example into the Egyptian myth of Isis and Osiris, or she may explore the pathway of ceremonial magic. In Wicca she will have been awakened to the vast possibilities that she can explore both with her body and her mind.

❦ 6 ❦
The Practice
of the Craft

Witches use the word 'work' to describe their activities and thus a solo magical operation or a group meeting becomes a 'working'. If a witch says that she will work for someone, it means that she will effect a healing spell or perhaps charge a talisman. A later chapter will discuss the pattern of the Pagan year, which is divided into eight major festivals known as the Sabbats, but being a witch involves more than occasional observance on specific dates. The real witch is involved in the Craft on a daily basis and to such an extent that it becomes part of the totality of her existence. She may meet with others on certain occasions, but in the privacy of her room and at her altar she is the priestess of the mysteries by night and day.

Ly Warren-Clarke is an Australian priestess who in the prologue to her book, *The Way of the Goddess*, has written a moving description of a true witch at work, capturing the mystery that is normally so difficult to describe as she prepares herself for magic.

'Her shapeless dress is unbuttoned and dropped to the floor; her hair, bound around her head in a tight braid, is unravelled and spreads around her in a burnished copper haze. The medallion she takes lovingly within her hands and greets with a soft kiss before raising it to the Moon's glow for approval; then she drops it over her head onto her breast drawing comfort from its familiar coldness on her skin.

'She kneels, raises her arms above her head, breathes deeply and waits. Very soon the Moon is fully risen and the shafts of silver cover her body and radiate around her. She cries out, in the ancient tongue of the Lands of Lirien, then she is ready to greet the Goddess, whose name rings around her thrice, like the chiming of bells.'

The passage goes on to describe the witch taking her cup and sprinkling her circle as she hums a soft melodious chant, building up a ring of mystic fire. Then she breathes in the smoke of the incense, summons the Four Winds to guard her circle by holding aloft the pentacle and presses her ritual knife to her breast.

'Her breath is still, the night is still. The forces of Life wait expectantly and suddenly the light returns to flood the room and the Priestess of the Moon cries out to the primordial Mother, to whom she was bequeathed before the Dawn of Time. The Mother answers with the heartbreak of a thousand, million lives and acknowledges the Child. They fuse and are one, the cycle is complete, and the Priestess of the Moon is assured: the Magic of her fingers will soothe where they lay, the Magic of her voice will heal where it is heard, the Magic of her eyes will light the Earth and all things will grow wherever she looks upon them.'

A number of distinctive Wiccan practices continue to attract controversy, not least ritual nakedness, which is invariably advanced by the popular press as evidence of irredeemable wickedness. Yet the majority of Wiccans prefer to work naked, or 'skyclad' as they call it, and believe that this is something completely natural. On the other hand, there are covens who wear robes for their gatherings, although even they would insist on a candidate for initiation being naked. However, even the most ardent disciples of skyclad working are often defeated by the vagaries of the British climate and wear cloaks or robes when out of doors. Shamanistic groups, who are essentially outdoor types, usually wear some form of clothing, and the ceremonial magicians favour ornate robes, headdresses and pendants. Ceremonial magic, by its very nature, relies heavily on the symbolism of colour which for certain types of working has to be reflected in the attire of the celebrants. Whether robed or naked, all are united in insisting on cleanliness before a working and not wearing ordinary street clothing.

Gerald Gardner was a practising naturist and a member of a club. This may have influenced his views, but ritual nudity has ancient roots in the mystery religions of Greece and elsewhere. According to Doreen Valiente, the original Gardner coven always worked naked. In the Charge or instruction in the *Book of Shadows* it states; 'And ye shall be free from slavery; and as a sign that ye be really free, ye shall be naked in your rites.' Gardner plagiarized this passage from Leland's book, *Aradia: The Gospel of the Witches*, and subsequently it has assumed the status of holy writ among many Wiccans.

In the minds of many readers of the tabloid press, nakedness is synonymous with sexual titillation, the result of orthodox religions' fear of sexuality. When Adam and Eve ate of the fruit of the tree they realized that they were naked and, as a result, God expelled them from the Garden of Eden. There are a number of reasons given by witches for their preference for working naked. As they believe in the sanctity of both spirit and body, they do not accept that anything to do with the latter is in any sense shameful. Thus their nakedness is an open acknowledgement of this duality and an expression of freedom from the shackles of religious convention. Very important is the democratic principle, as most people express how they would like others to view them by their choice of clothing and ornamentation. The fashion industry is geared to underpinning the human need for self-display, and hemlines rise and fall with monotonous regularity. When a number of witches come together and undress before entering the circle, they remove the symbols which can signify wealth, social status, class identification or even personal eccentricity. True equality within the circle is possible when everyone, whether rich or poor, is in the same state of freedom. On another democratic note, skyclad working dispenses with the ornate robes and accoutrements which attract some people to the occult while affirming that no amount of dressing up can provide a passport to effective psychic ability.

In psychological terms, writers on the Craft point out that to be effective a witch must come to terms with his or her own personality. This ability to see through the mask of the ego and forego the protective armour of clothing is often difficult to attain. Several witches I have spoken to have admitted that the most difficult hurdle for them to overcome was to undress for the first time and appear naked in front of others who they only previously knew when clothed. Men are worried that they might get an erection. Yet they all attest to the delight they felt once they had crossed that vital threshold and had experienced the freedom of being naked with their equals.

Another reason evinced to justify skyclad working is that it is said to be easier to raise psychic power when naked. Clearly, this is difficult to prove, but those with experience in the field firmly believe it.

The human body gives off static electricity, which was identified by Wilhelm Reich as 'orgone'. It might equally well be characterized as the animal magnetism which surrounds each of us with a particular aura or field of energy. This aura can be seen under certain circumstances and is a valuable diagnostic tool for many alternative therapists and healers. A healthy person has an evenly developed aura which is a pure light blue in colour, while the aura of someone who is unwell takes on an uneven shape and changes colour to reflect reds and pinks. The human aura can be pictured with a technique pioneered in Russian and known as Kirlian photography, which makes use of the bioplasmic energy surrounding every living thing. Therapists who use the aura for diagnosis examine their patients naked, as clothing can inhibit their view of it, while witches believe that being naked makes it easier to work magic.

Janet and Stewart Farrar, who have run a successful coven for many years, have a succinct answer to the inhibitions many people have about nakedness: 'We have had skyclad witches from eighteen to their sixties; men, women, tall, short, fat, thin, plain, stunning, raven, golden and grey; and nobody seems to mind. If anything, the less handsome ones seems reassured by the emphasis on our common humanity which skyclad practice brings; finding themselves treated as equals, they may even achieve a new poise and thus start making more of themselves, discovering attractive potentialities which they did not know they possessed.'

The robes that are worn are simple, loose kaftan-like garments preferably made from natural materials like

cotton, wool or silk. The colour can reflect the personality of the individual wearer, as each one of us has
certain subconscious colour preferences; or can be
determined by the purpose of the working. Healing, for
instance, uses red or orange. Colours also have planetary
linkings and each one of the four elements has its own
colour; green symbolizes water. Particular groups may
adopt a unified colour and design for their robes. A black
cloak with a hood for outdoor working is also popular
with witches, which sadly might be misconstrued as
evidence of their evil intent. The real reason, however, is
a practical one: a black all-enveloping cloak can conceal
one's identity from unwelcome snoopers.

One article common to most Wiccans is the cord with
which their hands were bound at their initiation and
which they afterwards wear around their waists when
naked or use to gather in their robes. Jewellery is also
important and female witches traditionally wear a necklace in the circle and often a bracelet as well. Necklaces
of acorns, after the representations of the Goddess Diana
of Ephesus, are popular. Some High Priestesses wear a
silver headband adorned with a crescent moon and their
male counterparts have a copper or brass circlet with a
sun symbol. Everyone in the circle will also wear their
own personal pendant, usually in the form of a silver
pentagram or the Egyptian looped cross, the *ankh* or
symbol of eternity. A delight in exotic jewellery, usually
silver to symbolize the moon and thus the Goddess, is
a hallmark of the witch and often an easy method
of identification. This phenomenon has been gently sati-
rized by Terry Pratchett who has created the character of
Magrat, the young witch, who appears in some of his
Discworld fantasy novels.

Wicca is not a religion without churches, temples in
which the worshippers gather, although I am sure that in

the future some will be built. Many Pagans habitually work out of doors, especially those who follow the shamanistic path, and some Wiccan groups have access to a piece of land where they can work undisturbed. There is a strong desire among Pagans of all persuasions to have access to worship at the ancient sites such as Stonehenge and Avebury, but this is yet to become a practical possibility. Although Druids can perform their ceremonies at Tower Hill and Primrose Hill or on top of Glastonbury Tor, anything associated with witchcraft still meets a wall of prejudice. As a result, most Wiccan groups, covens and solo witches have to work indoors in houses and flats, especially in winter.

All that is required is an area of unencumbered floor sufficiently large to accomodate the number of persons who will be present. Most witches use a living room as their temple from time to time, shifting the furniture out of the way. As far as equipment is concerned, the only requirement is for an altar, which can be a small table, a cupboard or a wooden chest. This is normally in permanent use as a house shrine and is simply moved to the north quadrant of the circle before a working. Those with sufficient space can dedicate a separate room as a temple and use it for this sole purpose. I have met witches who live in bedsits but still manage to create a magical atmosphere around their little shrines, as witchery is a matter of aptitude not money.

At the start of a working a witch casts a magical circle, creating a temple in what otherwise may be a mundane setting. In discussing what witches do and how they structure their worship, a number of generalizations are necessary owing to the individualistic approach to the Craft. There are, however, enough common features to provide a picture of Pagan worship based on a small coven working in an urban environment. The same problems would confront a writer attempting to define Christian worship in all its varieties from the Tridentine High Mass in a Gothic cathedral to a meeting of Plymouth Brethren in a corrugated tin chapel.

In Wiccan practice the altar is placed in the northern quadrant of the circle which is attributed to the element of earth. The other quadrants are east for air, south for fire and west for water. At each cardinal point a candle is placed which may be coloured according to the basic elemental symbolism – blue for the east, red for the south, green for the west and brown or orange for the north.

The altar is covered by a cloth and will have various items placed on it. There will be a statuette or representation of the Goddess, and perhaps of the God as well, and a vase of flowers. There will be at least one candlestick and a flat plate or pentacle on which a pentagram and other symbols are inscribed. A central feature is a cup or chalice for the communion, and containers for water and salt. Incense will be burned in a simple jossstick holder or a fine brass censer complete with chains like those in Catholic worship. Other items could include a wand, a bell, a symbolic scourge, a platter for a food offering and anything deemed important by the worshippers. Some covens own a fine sword and, in keeping with traditional country witchcraft, broomsticks and cauldrons are used for certain ceremonies. All the items of equipment used for a working, are consecrated and employed only in connection with ritual. Witches dislike anyone outside their own group handling ritual items.

The term 'working tools' is commonly used to define such items, and they are associated with the modern Craft rather than the ancient traditions of witches. For example, the four main tools of the ritual magicians, the sword, wand, cup and pentacle, corresponding to the four suits of the minor cards in a Tarot pack, come from the medieval *grimoires* of the Kabbalists. The items on the altar are usually the personal property of the witch or witches in whose house the working will take place. When obtaining such items, tradition demands that one must not haggle over the price; if one has the necessary skills it is preferable to make everything one-self. Witches often aquire working tools as gifts from like-minded friends and treasure them accordingly. Today it is possible to purchase a complete outfit from one of several suppliers of occult paraphernalia, a do-it-yourself witch kit. However, most of those I have spoken to have built up their own collection piecemeal, hunting in junk shops for such attractive items as old candlesticks and brass bells.

One item which is personal to each witch is a black-handled knife referred to as an *athame* (pronounced ath-ay-may), a term whose origin is obscure. The *athame* is traditionally given to a new initiate and consecrated as an integral part of the ceremony. Gerald Gardner specified the inscribing or carving of certain symbols on the handle, which he copied from an old *grimoire, The Key of Solomon the King. Athames* are usually ordinary sheath knives, kitchen knives or dagger-shaped ones purchased from occult suppliers. Together with the cord, the *athame* is taken by a witch to a meeting and is a symbol of his or her adherence. The *athame* is never used for cutting anything, and some witches have a separate white-handled knife for carving symbols on candles and wands.

It is difficult to estimate the percentage of witches who work in covens as opposed to those who work alone, with a partner or a couple of friends. Some covens claim direct descent through initiation from

Gerald Gardner's group, and the same applies naturally to the Alexandrians. There are also hereditary covens which lay claim to great antiquity through a particular family bond. Many modern covens have evolved around a couple who have initiated themselves and then brought in others. Some covens work in total secrecy while others openly advertise their existence and offer tuition leading to initiation.

Ideally a coven is led by a High Priestess with her male consort, husband or partner as the High Priest. These are not elective positions and are held by the incumbents for as long as the other members will accept them. Generally speaking, covens evolve around a particular couple who take on the priestly role and attract a group of followers. Leadership is practised by example and if the quality of that leadership is poor the followers will vote with their feet. The successful covens have a High Priestess who is skilled in magical matters, is a good teacher and can motivate the members. She needs to be a diplomat, have great powers of discretion and have a sense of humour. Her male counterpart, the High Priest, needs the same qualities as well as the ability to defer in matters spiritual to the High Priestess. In some covens the leadership is dominated by the male principle but they tend to have a high turnover of members. Any lack of balance and harmony between male and female has the potential to cause turbulence and is the main reason why covens periodically break up. In many groups there is a female witch known as the Maid or Maiden, who acts as assistant to the High Priestess in ritual matters. She is usually being groomed to take a higher degree and ultimately to form her own coven.

When a coven becomes too large, a section will 'hive off' and leave to form a new one. In the Gardnerian tradition any Second Degree witch can form a new coven subject to the approval and the supervision of the original High Priestess. A Third Degree witch is entitled to total independence. As a relic from the times of persecution, the same tradition lays down that the covenstead, or meeting place of the new group, should be at least three miles from that of the original coven. This is called voiding the coven, as in theory all contact between the new and the old should be broken off to enable the embryo group to build up its own group ethos. In large towns this is a practical impossibility and there is inevitably some overlap when a successful coven spawns a number of new ones over a period of years.

Ideally a coven should contain an equal number of men and women, who are paired off as couples to provide perfect sexual polarity. In practice this is seldom achieved and in a typical coven there will probably be a predominance of females. This is another potential source of trouble, particularly when personal relationships become strained. A rogue male who fancies himself can cause havoc, as can the man-eating female. Witches are only human, and the close proximity of working in the circle can lead to personal tensions and sexual dalliance. A good High Priestess should be able to nip such trouble in the bud.

In addition to the eight great festivals, covens traditionally meet on the night of the full moon, following the twenty-eight day cycle. Such a meeting is called an *esbat*, but the members can also come together on other occasions for specific purposes. An example might be the illness of a close relative of one of the members who will request a healing working to be performed. Individual witches can also follow a programme of activities in their own homes, and a High Priestess may hold training sessions for her less experienced members.

Let us observe a typical *esbat* held at the home of a High Priestess working in a town setting and within the mainstream of the Wiccan tradition. On the appointed night the members will gather at the house, bringing with them a bottle of wine and perhaps some food to share. On arrival there will be much hugging and kissing, as witches are physically affectionate, and gossip will be shared. Then the working space is cleared and the tools set out on the altar. If the High Priest and Priestess have children, they will have to check that they are tucked up in bed and fast asleep. Next clothes are shed and cords tied around waists in preparation for the ritual. The candles are lit, the incense burner started and all except the High Priestess and High Priest stand outside the area to the north-east.

The first part of any ritual working is the casting of the circle, which creates the boundary between the outside world and the participants, encasing them in a bubble that protects them from any harm. The idea of working within a magic circle is common to most ancient religious traditions. The High Priestess and High Priest kneel in front of the altar, and she places a bowl of water on the pentacle. Dipping the blade of her *athame* into the bowl, she consecrates the water and places the bowl to one side. The High Priest then takes the pot of salt, places it on the pentacle and consecrates it in the same way with the tip of his *athame*. Taking a pinch of the salt, he sprinkles it into the water, transforming it into a purifying agent.

The High Priestess takes her *athame*, or a sword if she has one; starting in the east, she draws a circle clockwise or deosil, leaving a gateway in the north-east. As she moves around she draws in the astral power through the crown of her head, imagining it flowing down her arm and out through the point of the *athame* as an

Sir Francis Dashwood, founder of the Hell Fire Club, dressed as a monk worshipping Venus (*Mansell Collection*)

Aleister Crowley, the self-styled Master Therion, the Great Beast, 666 of
the *Book of Revelations* (*Mary Evans*)

Tarot cards used in divination. A pack consists of four suits of the
so-called Minor Arcana, Wands, Swords, Pentacles and Cups each card
representing an archetype (*Hugh Gulland*)

Frontispiece from a modern wiccan grimoire of the Arcadia type copied
from Charles Godfrey Leyland's *Arcadia, or Gospel of Witches* 1899
(*Charles Walker*)

Cornish witches invoking the 'Owlman' near Falmouth in 1980
(*Anthony Shiels/Fortean picture Library*)

The Druid Stone on the Great Orme, Gwynedd, known locally as the
Maen Sigl (*Charles Walker*)

Sky-clad woman with a ritual dagger held over a chalice in a sexual
ritual (*Charles Walker*)

The Cornish Witch Caith Sidh (*Fortean Picture Library*)

Ritual implements at a sabbat, or witch festival, candles, skull, grimoire, rod and sword (*Charles Walker*)

Witch in the ritual of 'drawing down the moon' with the sacred sword
(*Charles Walker*)

intense blue light which envelops the working area. She then replaces the sword or knife on the altar and admits the other members into the circle with a kiss, sealing the north-east gateway with the *athame* after the last person has entered.

The High Priestess can delegate the casting of the circle or any other part of the ritual to another female witch, and any male witch can assume the role of the High Priest for the occasion. In this way a good coven leader who does not suffer from an over-inflated sense of her own importance will ensure that all her witches gain the experience they will need to run their own circle.

Next the circle is strengthened by the addition of elemental symbolism. One witch carries the bowl of consecrated salt and water clockwise around the circle, sprinkling the perimeter as she goes and then sprinkling each of the participants before returning the bowl to the altar. She is followed by a second witch who carries the incense burner and a third witch carrying the altar candle: earth, water, air and fire. Finally, the four watchtowers or guardian presences are invoked, a ritual practice adopted from the ceremonial magicians of the Golden Dawn. All those present take their *athames* and stand behind the High Priestess who faces towards the east. She draws an invoking pentagram with her blade, imagining it as a flaming shape while the others copy her movements. As she does so she calls out:

Ye Lords and Watchtowers of the east, Lords of Air. I do summon, stir and call you up to witness these our rites and to guard our circle.

The pentagrams and the invocation are repeated for the south, the west and the north. Some witches do not like the implications of 'summoning' such mighty entities and prefer more humbly to request their presence.

To some this may appear to be no more than empty ritual posturing, as indeed it is in the hands of the inexperienced and poorly taught. The skilled magician visualizes each step and can fix in his or her imagination the glowing circle of fire and the flaming pentagrams at each quarter which enclose the participants in a powerful protective cage. Visualization is also needed at the next stage of the ritual, known as Drawing down the Moon, in which the High Priest invokes the Goddess within the High Priestess. This is an act of worship which can be carried out only by a man who has been able to cast aside all male chauvinism. It is not just a question of repeating the words and actions; he must be able to visualize the transformation as the woman he knows as Mary, Jane or Liz in everyday life takes on the aspects of the Goddess.

The High Priestess stands with her back to the altar holding the wand in her right hand and the scourge in her left. She crosses her hands over her breasts to form the Osiris position. (The Egyptian God of that name is often pictured with his symbols of the crook and flail standing in this posture.) The High Priest kneels before her and gives her the five-fold kiss described in the chapter on initiation. As he reaches her breasts she opens out her arms and for the kiss on the lips they touch their bodies together full length. The High Priest then returns to the kneeling position and looking up at his High Priestess invokes the Goddess to descend into her.

With the protective circle drawn and the presence of the Goddess incarnate within the High Priestess, she proceeds to declaim the Charge or instruction quoted in full in the chapter on the deities. Its purpose is to remind the members of the coven of their fundamental beliefs; ideally it should be spoken from memory rather than being read out. The final parts of the opening ritual consist of the High Priest invoking the presence of the God within the circle and a round dance accompanied by a chant which Gardner called the Witch's Rune. In ancient times Pagans danced and chanted, and it is an excellent way of charging the atmosphere.

It must be stressed that the basic opening ritual is adapted by each coven from the original material in the *Book of Shadows*. While adhering to the structure, many covens and witches have rewritten the ritual to remove some of the outlandish chants favoured by Gardner, seemingly on the grounds that if they were old they must be good. Many modern witches dislike using words which they do not understand but all would agree with the principle of working within a consecrated circle.

The next step is for the coven to proceed to the working which they wish to undertake. If all the members are well trained, they will be able naturally to focus their group mind on the object to be attained. The purposes for a working might include healing, making a spell to help someone to pass an examination or sorting out a marital difficulty. The person for whom the working is being undertaken may or may not know about it, and it does not matter if he or she does not believe in the powers of witchery. The only constraints imposed are those of the natural laws of magic and morality bound up with the law of three-fold return. Each participant takes on a share of the responsibility for the outcome of each and every magical act and thus careful consideration must be given to the objective of any working.

Divination might also be carried out on behalf of an individual or the coven as a whole. An example of the latter might be the discovery of a suitable date for the initiation of a new member, using Tarot, the I Ching or Rune stones. A full moon meeting can also be used for training purposes with the High Priestess leading a group meditation or visualization exercise.

The working period is followed by the communion, another element common to almost every religion, in which food and drink is shared by the worshippers. The practice probably originates in prehistoric times and the old Nature worship in which the members of a tribe thanked the Gods for the provision of nourishment from the earth. In the Wiccan ritual, the communion is also a celebration in token of the Great Rite of sexual polarity. A male witch takes the chalice of red wine from the altar and kneels, holding it, in front of a female witch. She takes the sword or her *athame* and, lowering the tip into the wine, says: 'As the sword is to the male, so is the cup to the female, and conjoined they bring blessedness.' As she performs this act she pulls down the astral power, letting it flow as a river of light into the wine, at the same time her male partner visualizes the same silvery light. The sexual symbolism is obvious and seen by witches as a celebration of the creative force in Nature. Of great significance in this ritual is the element of role reversal, with the man holding the cup, the symbol of the womb, and the woman taking the sword, the phallic emblem. This is in keeping with polarity and serves to emphasize the contra-sexual side in each human being.

Having consecrated the chalice, the female witch replaces the sword or *athame* on the altar and kneels before her partner. He kisses her and hands her the cup, from which she takes a sip. She then kisses him and hands back the cup, which is then passed around the circle from male to female and vice versa. A drop is always left in the bottom to be offered afterwards to the earth. This is followed by the blessing of the food, usually pieces of bread, small home-baked cakes or biscuits. These are laid out on a plate with one for each participant and an extra one for the earth offering. Again, a male witch takes the plate and, using her powers of visualization, a female draws a pentagram with her *athame* over it. The words used in the *Book of Shadows* come from Crowley's Gnostic Mass: 'O Queen most secret, bless this food into our bodies; bestowing health, wealth, strength, joy, and peace, and that fulfilment of love which is perfect happiness.'

After the communion ceremony there is time to relax within the circle. If powerful magic has been worked the participants will feel pleasantly drained and the sharing of food and wine is a valuable aid to earthing all concerned. Tension flows out and is replaced with the happiness of a powerful shared experience. The chalice is passed around and everyone can talk freely, still within the protective realm of the circle. The glow of the candlelight, and perhaps the warmth of an open fire, plays on the naked bodies relaxing and the smell of the incense lingers in the room. The sense of love and sharing with brothers and sisters brings a sense of contentment and spiritual fulfilment. Witchery differs from the established religions in that the participants do not have to be solemn and po-faced after a working. Relaxing in the circle is a chance for feasting, drinking and being merry in honour of the God and Goddess. Jokes can be told and the humour can become quite Rabelaisian while at the same time remaining within the bounds of good taste. I have yet to meet a miserable witch, and a sense of fun is vital to the practice of the

Craft. If something goes wrong during a working, the tendency is for everyone to burst into fits of laughter before starting again.

All that remains is for the circle to be closed down. The High Priestess again stands in the east with the rest of the coven behind her. She draws a banishing pentagram and at the same time visualizes it disappearing as if a light has been switched off. At the same time the Maiden, or another witch who has been appointed, blows out the east candle. The Guardian Lords of the east are thanked for their presence and requested to return to their fair dwellings with the words 'hail and farewell' which are repeated by all those present. This is repeated in the remaining three quarters, ending in the north in front of the altar, where the presiding deities are also thanked. In the final act the rest of the wine in the chalice and the extra cake or biscuit is taken outside into the garden for the offering to the earth. The wine is tipped out and the food is crumbled on to the soil, with thanks to the Gods for their gifts. If it is a clear night, the full moon will be high in the sky, shining down on the small group of naked people making their offering to the most ancient deities known to mankind. The witches will feel a powerful sense of communion with those powers and with the earth under their bare feet. Even the most urbanized of them will be at one with their spiritual roots.

This outline of a coven working at the full moon will apply equally to the solo witch, a couple or two friends working together. They too will cast their circle, carry out the work they have set themselves to perform and celebrate the communion. They will not enjoy the companionship of a coven, but some witches prefer to be on their own to avoid the internal differences which can sometimes split a coven. Even the most devoted coven members, however, will also engage in private witchery at home.

Some witches may devote time to such disciplines as yoga or tai chi, using them as forms of mental and physical training. Almost all regularly practise meditation to help with visualization and path working. Any school of occult training will advocate the need for the expansion of the imagination as one of the keys to the development of psychic ability. Divination is another regular form of magical activity and some witches will do readings for friends or even professionally. For the devotees of alternative medicine there are herbs to be gathered and dried and preparations to be made up; for those who are active as therapists, there are patients to be seen. For a witch the baking of bread, the preparation of wholesome food for the family, the brewing of beer and the fermenting of wine are considered as magical as studying books on esoteric theory. Being a witch is a full-time job whether at home, at work or among friends.

Rites of passage, the ritual celebration of birth, puberty, marriage and death, meet a deep-seated human need and are common to every religion. The *Book of Shadows* did not provide for such rituals and over the years Wiccans have developed their own. Several versions have been published, all of which are equally valid.

The Wiccan view of the rites of birth is diametrically opposed to that of Christianity, in which baptism by the priest or minister implies a lifelong commitment. Even if the ritual is carried out purely as a social obligation, the element of commitment is still there, coupled to the myth that an unbaptized child will go straight to Hell. Pagans also regard such customs as circumcision as a barbaric form of child abuse. During a recent radio programme upon the subject of 'ritual abuse', a witch who was participating commented that if Pagans removed extraneous bits of their children's bodies as part of a religious ceremony there would soon be an outcry.

The ceremony used by witches is sometimes referred to as Wiccaning and is in reality a form of dedication and naming of a child. It does not seek any commitment, purely asking for the gods to protect and guide the child until such time as it is old enough to choose its own religious path. The child is brought into the circle by its parents, anointed and given a name. In some traditions an additional hidden witch name is also given. If the parents so wish, sponsors or godparents may be chosen who promise to guide the child and act as its friends. Afterwards gifts are given to the child and all those present join in a small celebration. Similar rituals were developed by the New Age travellers who brought their children to be named at Stonehenge on the morning of the Summer Solstice, in the days before they were banned from the monument. I know of several cases where parents who sympathize with Paganism have asked Wiccans to conduct ritual dedications for their children.

The next traditional rite of passage in the life of the individual occurs at puberty, when a young person is officially recognized as an adult within the tribe or social grouping. In the Christian churches this is marked by confirmation, at which the candidate reaffirms the promises made on his or her behalf at baptism and can afterwards partake in the ritual communion. Wicca has made no provision for such a rite for the simple reason that children are not involved in magical work-ing and covens do not initiate people who are minors. However, as a more open view of Paganism takes root, such attitudes will inevitably change. Children who are brought up in Pagan households will gain an insight into the beliefs of their parents and their parents' friends. No responsible person would involve a child in a magical working, but purely ceremonial occasions, such as Yule, should be family occasions. As increasing numbers of children grow up in Pagan and Wiccan families, the need for a rite at puberty may well evolve of its own accord.

A witch wedding is known as a handfasting and, again, no specific ritual is laid down. Several have been published and many couples devise their own. Such a ceremony is not legally binding, but for witches who believe in the reality of magic it is not to be entered into lightly. It cannot be annulled by employing a solicitor and applying to a court of law. In most cases a couple will already be established lovers when they reach the point in their relationship at which they wish to make a firm and binding commitment within their beliefs. If the couple are members of a coven, the ceremony will be performed by the High Priest and Priestess according to their normal practice. It is a time for celebration and both bride and groom can wear special robes, although they will both approach the altar naked. In keeping with Wiccan beliefs, the marriage can be consummated within the circle after the other members of the coven have left. The rite ends with a merry jumping over the broomstick and a happy party.

Finally, there is death, which to Pagans who believe in reincarnation is not something to inspire terror. The one who has departed has left for the Summerlands, the fairy realm in the west where he or she will be refreshed before the cycle of rebirth starts again. The Farrars have published a ritual, which they call a requiem, for performance within a coven in remembrance of a member who has died. This is not a funeral service, which must be carried out in a public place such as a crematorium. Pagan funerals have caused some controversy in the past but are more common today as old prejudices are gradually broken down. When Alex Sanders died, his friends organized a service at Hastings crematorium at which incense was burned and soft music played on a guitar. As crematoria are generally municipally owned and their chapels non-denominational, Pagans have the right to conduct ceremonies within the guidelines laid down by the authorities.

The following is taken from a recent article in *The Wiccan*, the magazine of the Pagan Federation, written by John Ruse and entitled Requiem for Nicola, a ten-year-old girl. Her parents asked the author to conduct a service at the crematorium. He wrote that he received unstinting help from both the undertaker and the director of the crematorium, although the former was slightly bewildered at first. The burning of incense, lighting candles and playing the music of the parents' choice was arranged with sympathy and understanding. The only hitch occurred when 'a certain so-called Christian minister attempted to disrupt the funeral of a child by telephoning the crematorium authorities, and claiming that Nicola's father was involved with Black Magic'.

This was dismissed by the official concerned and the staff removed a Christian cross from the chapel before the service without having to be asked. They even helped to light the candles and place them on the coffin. This extract from the service illustrates Pagan belief about death.

We commend Nicola to the love and care of the Lord and Lady, and the Great Mother.

We pray that her passage be smooth and that the Light Bearer illuminate her path; that the handmaidens of the Goddess lead her gently by the hand and that the Gods protect her.

Nicola left us with the gift of simplicity and trust that only a child can bestow. She stepped into the darkness of the Goddess's embrace without fear. One day we must all follow her along that path. May we share some of that innocence and trust and knowledge that after the darkness follows the light. Death as we know it is but a transition — an initiation.

❦ 7 ❦
Sociology of Witchcraft

I n attempting to define who witches and Pagan folk are, the backgrounds from which they come and their views on a number of important social issues — what might be termed the sociology of witchcraft — one is bedevilled by a lack of reliable statistics. I make no apology, therefore, for basing this chapter on personal opinion based on empirical observation. There is no such thing as a typical witch, or even a typical Pagan, and those wishing to make contact with the practitioners of the Old Religion cannot find them in the Yellow Pages.

Popular prejudice against witchcraft has compelled many Pagans to conceal their beliefs for fear of discrimination at work and in the community. They might also be apprehensive about the attitude towards their children adopted by teachers and social workers. It is a paradox that in Britain the main political parties have all courted the Muslim vote and subscribe to the notion that we live a multi-cultural society. A so-called parliament has recently been formed by a vociferous section of the Muslim community and not a single prosecution has been instigated against those who publicly endorsed the death sentence imposed upon the unfortunate Salman Rushdie. Pagans feel that the exercise of these double standards, in a supposedly free society, have placed them on the defensive, and only recently have some of them begun to fight back.

To the best of my knowledge the only statistical analysis of Paganism was published in 1989 as *The Occult Census*, the result of a sample of slightly over 1,000 replies to a questionnaire. This is a respectable sample and consistent with the numbers used by professional pollsters trying to predict the results of the next general election. The survey originated in 1988 as a result of the Reachout campaign against the supposed connection between witchcraft and child abuse which was subsequently proved to be totally unfounded. Chris Bray, the proprietor of a retail and mail order occult supply business in Leeds, The Sorcerer's Apprentice, and a veteran campaigner against those who defame the occult distributed the questionnaires through organizations, groups, magazines and individuals. He issued the results in the form of a booklet and, by extrapolating his figures against official population surveys, came up with a total of 250,000 practising occultists in Britain. Almost 70 per cent of those polled stated that they were witches or Pagans, producing a figure of 200,000. At the time of writing there is every reason to believe that the figure is now considerably higher. Since the survey was completed there has been a spate of new publications on the Craft, and the membership of such groups as the Pagan Federation demonstrate a marked upward curve.

Examination of the figures in *The Occult Census* shows that 67 per cent of those questioned became interested in the occult at about the age of seventeen or earlier and that the average age of those polled was twenty-seven. One can deduce from this that the majority of today's occultists were born in the 1960s and grew up in that heady time. 37 per cent of them had received some form of higher education and a further 21 per cent had university degrees. Only 10 per cent considered themselves unemployed and the vast majority were engaged in respectable and responsible vocations, including journalism, nursing, the civil service, engineering, computer-related activities and management. The survey demonstrated conclusively that the occult was not the prerogative of an unlettered underclass of drop-outs.

My own experience bears out the truth of these statistics. The majority of witches I have met are in their thirties, own their own homes, live in a state of stable coupledom and have two children. Both partners are likely to be employed in a responsible although not necessarily highly paid job. They do not openly flout the laws of the land, but pay their taxes and probably vote for the Green Party. The pursuit of private wealth which characterized the 1980s passed them them by and they would not regard themselves as members of the consumer society. The majority are vegetarians, dislike wearing man-made fibres and, indeed, abhor 'fashion'. Their children are open-minded and are encouraged to speak out rather than blindly accept the dictates of their peer group.

There is a younger faction and its members are equally non-conformist. They are generally to be found at alternative Rock festivals, browsing round the shops at Glastonbury and drinking in the pubs of bed-sitter land. There are few rich witches. The flaunting of status symbols is alien to Pagans as much of their ethos is ecological. Favourite modes of transport include the Citroen 2cv, old post-office vans and bicycles. They will, however, spend their money on more expensive biological washing powder and eat wholefoods rather than junk. As there is no salaried Pagan hierarchy of priests or officials, there is no financial reward for membership of the Craft, although some gain their living by related activities, notably as the proprietors of shops selling incense, clothing, books, jewellery and occult paraphernalia. These often act as rallying points for local Pagans who can equally be found in the local vegetarian café or shopping at street markets. Some Pagans practise as alternative therapists and healers, offering a variety of treatments throughout the range of fringe medicine. Some Pagans offer their services as astrologers or give Tarot readings; they do not like to be confused with fortune tellers.

One of the principles of witchy philosophy is that it is improper to charge for services of a magical nature. One cannot take money for working a spell. Some witches extend this principle to Tarot readings, refusing to accept a fee, although they might take a gift in kind. Some healers ask for a donation rather than set a fixed scale of fees for consultations. Even a healer or a Tarot reader has to live, but this vexed question can cause a lot of heartache, especially to people who would prefer a barter economy. There are, for example, a wide variety of small-scale publications catering for the Pagan world and usually run by someone as a hobby and financed by subscriptions. They enable people to keep in touch, advertise alternative music venues, courses and workshops, and are sometimes a vehicle for the editor to pursue his own particular hobby-horse. Pagans can also earn a modest living by producing Craft items or works of art. Painters, wood carvers, wand makers and candle suppliers, satisfy the Pagan preference for handmade items over mass-produced things.

Popular prejudice has obliged many witches to conceal their belief from neighbours, colleagues at work and teachers or social workers who may be in contact with their children. A teacher who is a witch, for example, could face grave problems if parents found out and informed the local education authority and the press. Covert witches display no occult items, such as a shrine, in their homes and tend to socialize with their own kind. Initiation into a coven involves a vow of secrecy, binding the candidate never to reveal the names and addresses of other members to outsiders. Sadly this remains a necessary precaution and many witches are frightened to 'come out'.

Pagans, rather than witches, can more easily talk openly about their beliefs as the public does not automatically associate them with Devil worship or child abuse. In the privacy of their homes evidence of their beliefs is discernible, although always understated: the lingering smell of incense, a small table in a corner with a candlestick, vase of flowers and a statuette of a naked female, will subtly inform those in the know. Some openness is required of coven leaders, who must be prepared to meet genuine applicants for membership. As a journalist I was treated with great caution by many witches until I was able to convince them that I was not setting out to write yet another exposé of their wickedness.

Writers can always hide behind their publishers' and most will answer letters from readers which are passed on to them. The Pagan Federation has a London box number and some of its activists correspond with enquirers using assumed names. Those who write for the various Pagan magazines also often use pseudonyms to protect their real identities and can only be contacted through the editor. As such publications have a limited circulation and are only advertised in occult circles, those who appear openly in them have little to fear. At the end of her book on Wicca, Vivienne Crowley gives a box number where she can be contacted, and the Farrars have courageously given their home address in Ireland in their books.

In the past making contact was extremely difficult, but now there are several organizations, listed at the end of this book, where enquirers can be passed on to someone in their neighbourhood. Generally speaking, witches with a middle-class lifestyle in a well-to-do neighbourhood are more likely to keep their heads down. A youngster living in a bed-sit surrounded by other alternative types has less to fear and can openly appear in a billowing dress and occult jewellery.

In addition covert and semi-covert witches there is a third and highly controversial category: the self-publicists who enjoy a high public profile and frequent notoriety. Such people have always been attracted by the mystical side of the Craft and its potential for theatricality. Both Gardner and Saunders were prepared to give interviews and the subsequent distortions and half-truths that emerged were usually counter-productive. Orthodox witchery has always disapproved of those who have pushed themselves forward or have claimed to act as spokespersons on the Craft. One could call this the 'rentawitch' syndrome, and every tabloid journalist has the phone number of a co-operative witch in his contact book. It is only comparatively recently that leading figures in the Craft have begun to make themselves available to responsible journalists. Nevertheless, every request for an interview is still treated with the deepest suspicion.

Kevin Carlyon, a witch based in Eastbourne, Sussex, has received regular coverage in the popular press for some years and equally regular condemnation from the local clergy. Carlyon calls his brand of the Craft the Covenant of Earth Magic and, together with his wife Ingrid, runs a small group which has even made a video for sale to enquirers. Always respectably robed, at least for press photographers, the Carlyons have pulled number of spectacular stunts. The headline to an article in *The Guardian* on 6 May, 1989, reads: 'BR faces a spell of trouble from witches and ley lines'. This referred to a ritual inspired by the Carlyons to force British Rail to move the route of the proposed Channel Tunnel Link as it threatened to pass through Kits Coty, an ancient megalithic site in Kent. The article also stated that the coven had been successful in charming foxes out of a chicken run and woodpeckers out of the beehives of a local farmer.

Far more controversial was a much-publicized ritual against the Poll Tax which was performed in March 1990 on the slopes of another ancient site in Sussex, the Long Man of Wilmington. This involved burning the effigies of Mrs Thatcher, the late MP, Ian Gow, the leader of the council and the local mayor. Kevin Carlyon stated that the purpose was to use the positive thoughts created at the ritual to persuade the government to drop the Poll Tax. Well, they did, so perhaps the magic worked. Activity of this kind, if not outright black magic, is certainly extremely grey and can only harm the cause of Paganism. On the positive side, the Carlyons, by having the courage to publicize their work, bring the knowledge of the existence of the Craft to a wider public. Nevertheless, serious witches would prefer Kevin Carlyon to restrict his efforts to banning woodpeckers from beehives.

Organization in the Pagan world has always been a contentious subject as so many practitioners resent any attempt to lay down guidelines and form ruling committees. As the essence of Pagan thought is bound up with freedom from hierarchical religious structures, many are suspicious of any organization set up to represent them. But as the number of Pagans increases, as do the attacks against them, there is a growing groundswell of opinion that the movement needs a coherent structure. As the Universal Declaration of Human Rights guarantees freedom of religion, some Pagans believe that their beliefs should be recognized as a 'religion'.

The responsible voice of Paganism in Britain is the Pagan Federation, which was founded in 1971. Originally it was a mainly Wiccan organization which was set up at the height of the sometimes vicious inter-faction quarrels between the Gardnerians and the Alexandrians. Although its quarterly magazine is still called *The Wiccan*, the Federation has developed to provide a platform for Druids, shamans, Dianic witches and those working in the Nordic tradition. It has a lively correspondence with overseas Pagans and has established contact with the newly liberated Baltic States. Its elected committee holds an annual conference attended by a lively membership which has largely thrown off the lunatic fringe. The Federation speaks to the media on behalf of Paganism and has produced a booklet refuting the claims of ritual sexual abuse by witches.

No movement is immune from factionalism stirred by minor pressure groups which often become the most vociferous and unrepresentative. The influence of Communists in the trade union movement provides a good example. In 1988 a combination of militant

feminists and anarchists attempted to hijack the proceedings at a Paganlink conference held in Sheffield.
The conference was wrecked, but Paganlink weathered
the storm and continues as a valuable means of putting
Pagans in touch with each other.

Strident factionalism strikes at the very harmony
prized by the Pagan community. Anarchists have always
been on the fringes of the Pagan movement and are
strongly represented among the ranks of the New Age
travellers where attitudes have been hardened by police
brutality. Wicca has easily absorbed the contribution
made by Dianic beliefs and can accommodate the need
for women to celebrate their mysteries amongst themselves. Some Dianic groups exclude men while others
are happy to work with men who are in sympathy with
their aims. Militant feminism, on the other hand has no
place, either within the Craft or Paganism, as its philosophy is directly opposed to the central belief in
male/female polarity. By the same token, the belief in
male/female polarity excludes male homosexuals. Some
Wiccan writers state openly that they would find it difficult to work with gay people. In the United States
there are male homosexual covens which claim to be
Wiccan, but it is difficult to see how they can make
magic in this tradition. In Britain there is an association
called Hoblink which acts as a contact network for gay
and bisexual Pagans.

One widespread organisation which cuts across many
of the divisions within the Pagan world is the Fellowship
of Isis, which has over 11,000 members in seventy-two
countries. It is run by Olivia Robertson and her brother,
Lawrence, Lord Strathloch, from Clonegal Castle in
Ireland. The aim of the Fellowship is to restore the
veneration of the Goddess in her many forms, using
the name of Isis, which is the oldest and most popular.

The Robertsons have produced a number of booklets on a Goddess-oriented liturgy and ordain members to the priesthood of Isis.

The use of drugs sparks a great deal of controversy. Mainstream Wiccans are strongly opposed to the use of drugs, pointing out that a good magician needs no artificial substance to channel power or to influence imagination. Nevertheless, from the earliest times drugs have played a role in religious traditions, inducing trance states and promoting visionary experiences. Most shamanistic traditions use hallucinogenic substances. Aleister Crowley consumed a variety of drugs throughout his life, as have many other visionaries in the history of the occult. Some witches cultivate a couple of healthy cannabis plants in a discreet corner of the garden behind the compost heap. Many Pagans support the movement to legalize cannabis. A significant proportion of Pagans smoke pot socially, a far less socially damaging activity than the over-consumption of lager on a Friday night. Books are available on 'legal highs' and many Pagans look forward to the autumnal harvest of 'magic mushrooms' as part of the bounty of Mother Earth. There is, however, general agreement that the use of 'hard' and addictive substances is not compatible with the Pagan viewpoint. Drug abuse has always been one of the sticks used to beat the New Age travellers and the Free Festival movement and the justification of much unnecessary police repression. The Flower Power revolution that spread to Europe from California in the 1960s was permeated by the pleasures of a joint shared around the fire and many found that controlled taking of LSD produced a mind-enhancing experience. While the elders of the Craft, and society as a whole, may frown on drug consumption, it is a fact that substances will be openly on sale at alternative music festivals where

New Age folk gather and there will be no shortage of customers.

Meat eating is a topic which generates fierce debate among Pagans, which is reflected in the correspondence section of *The Wiccan*. The vegetarian lobby is probably in the ascendant, together with the more extreme Vegans who eschew all animal products, even wool pullovers and leather footwear. Tina Fox, who runs an organization called Pagan Animal Rights, is a tireless campaigner who points out the hypocrisy, common in the Pagan movement, 'of professing care and concern for Nature and then exploiting Her creatures'. The meat-eaters counter by claiming that humans are natural carnivores and that plants are alive as well. The consumption of meat is given a gloss of respectability by those who will only buy organic products from specialist butchers, free range eggs and eschew factory-farmed products. Others, who have the space, are prepared to rear and slaughter their own animals in the most humane conditions. What does seem to unite all Pagans is strong opposition to hunting and bloodsports, the keeping of animals in inhumane conditions and their exploitation in unnecessary scientific experimentation.

It has been stated that Wiccan covens do not initiate those under eighteen and some set an even higher age limit for admission. What approach should witches adopt to their own children? The attitude of the Pagan Federation has recently been set out in a booklet entitled *Something out of Nothing*, which deals with the vexed question of child abuse, and I quote from an article therein.

'To Pagans and Wiccans, children are very special. They are our future; our life depends to a great extent on them growing up sound in body and mind and with respect for their fellows and the world on which they live. To mistreat a child, in any way at all, is sowing the seeds of cruelty, abuse and mental instability in future generations. . . Unlike many, Pagans and Wiccans do not believe in imposing their own beliefs on their children. . . Pagan parents raise their children to have a deep respect for life and nature in all its forms. A child brought up in a Pagan family is taught that all natural things are sacred, that the ideas and the beliefs of others are to be tolerated and not attacked. They are taught to respect the property of others whether private or public, encouraged to look for the good in all things and to stand up against what is bad.'

That would seem to be a reasonable set of ethics which all parents, not necessarily Pagan, should aim for.

Another factor is naturally the archetypal image, based on known history, of the witch as the village healer and the shaman as medicine man.

Alternative medicine is a topic of interest to all Pagans. Most would agree that not all medical doctors over-prescribe drugs for their patients, but Pagans harbour a deep suspicion of the motives and methods of the medical profession. This will not prevent them from seeking treatment from their doctor, particularly if they have something mechanical wrong with them, but they will only accept a prescribed form of treatment if they are convinced that it is necessary. No amount of magic will fix a broken leg.

Not all alternative therapists are Pagans and there are many successful Christian practitioners. The ethos of healing, however, is located very close to the Pagan interest in the powers of Nature and the realization that much illness is in the mind rather than the body.

Much of the regular magical work of a coven and that of an individual witch is concerned with healing on the spiritual plane by using the powers of concentration and imagination. Additionally, many witches prepare their own herbal remedies and offer practical healing by the laying on of hands, massage and aromatherapy. Some have greater ability than others and may go on to study a particular method with the aim of gaining a qualification and practising publicly. There are others who have qualified in psychology and who are active as counsellors, finding that the academic discipline helps them as witches in their understanding of the workings of the mind. The field of natural healing is vast, containing a bewildering variety of therapies, but it is steadily gaining in popularity as people become dissatisfied with drug-related treatments which relieve the symptoms rather than looking at the cause.

If you are not a Pagan at heart, there will be several living just around the corner from you and probably a coven of witches which meets somewhere not too far away. You may not be able to spot them instantly, and the local High Priest will not sport a dog collar or a turban. They are not a threat to anyone's children nor are they busily cooking up Satanic spells. Their love of Nature and humanity is in keeping with the needs of the planet today. There are some eccentrics and drop-outs in their ranks, but no more than in any other cross-section of the community. Pagans ask only to be accorded the tolerance that is enshrined in law.

❦ 8 ❦

The Pagan Year

P agan worship revolves around a cycle of eight
festivals: four of them, the great Sabbats, are of
Celtic origin and the remainder are of astronomical significance.

Samhain (Hallowe'en)	31 October
Yule	22 December
Imbolc (Candlemas)	2 February
Spring Equinox	21 March
Beltaen	30 April
Summer Solstice	21 June
Lugnasadh (Lammas)	31 July
Autumn Equinox	21 September

The celebration of these festivals is common to
Wiccans, Druids and Pagans, all of whom follow the
natural movement of the seasons as their ancestors did
thousands of years ago. The same dates, however, often
coincide with the festivals of other ancient religions

which employed a similar mythological calendar, indicating the archetypal nature of seasonal observance. Some of them were Christianized and given new names or were taken over as saints' days as the leaders of the new religion discovered that the urge to worship at the times of the old festivals was too deeply ingrained to be eradicated by decree. As Nature has many aspects, so the festivals bring together a variety of themes common to all societies, particularly those which are agrarian. These themes include solar power, lunar and planetary influences, psychic themes, legend, planting and harvesting and animal husbandry. The dates of the lesser Sabbats, the two equinoxes and the two solstices, are determined by astronomical observation. These go back beyond the Celts to their Neolithic predecessors, who aligned their stone circles not only to reflect the changing seasons but also to act as astronomical calculators on which to base the cycle of planting and harvesting. The great Sabbats have traditional dates that are reflected in Celtic myth and are mirrored in similar traditions upheld by other ancient faiths.

The astronomical festivals are all solar — oriented fire festivals based on the cycle of the Sun God who is born in winter, rises through manhood into maturity and then fades into old age and dies, only to be reborn again the following year. The Great Sabbats are both lunar and goddess-oriented, revolving around the seasonal animal husbandry practised by our remote ancestors. The maiden goddess is impregnated by the young god, who is both her son and then lover, brings forth the child as mother and, as crone, presides over the death and rebirth of the year at Samhain. In the Greek mysteries she descends into the underworld in Autumn only to re-emerge in Spring as the life-giving maiden. Unlike the goddess, who is immortal, the god dies, to be born again year by year. This fertility cycle is paralleled in most of the ancient religions, although in modern witchcraft the yearly ritual slaughter of the High Priest is no longer fashionable.

Underlying the principle of the eight great festivals is a truth beyond the mere continuation of ancient traditions which is sometimes missed by those who celebrate them. As the year is cyclical, so is all of human life; and as Pagans accept reincarnation, death is but a transitory event leading to eventual rebirth. The seasons are linked to the sun which is reborn at the winter solstice, grows through the spring to reach its greatest power at midsummer and wanes in autumn. The sun never dies nor does the human being. As the sun is the centre of the annual cycle, so the spirit is the pole around which a human life moves. We are born, grow through adolescence into adulthood, reach our greatest strength, and then pass into the autumn of our lives on our way to death, only to repeat the cycle yet again. Thus the seasonal celebrations reflect our awareness of our essential humanity and give us a sense of our immortality entwined in the cycle of Nature. That could well explain the universal human need to mark the rites of passage with initiatory ceremonies to coincide with birth, puberty, marriage and death.

Gerald Gardner's *Book of Shadows* gave little detail on the seasonal observations, and many Wiccans use *Eight Sabbats for Witches*, by Janet and Stewart Farrar as a basis for the their own workings. Other sets of rituals have been published, but many Pagans prefer to devise their own. Wiccans, who usually work indoors, have adopted festivals and forms best suited to a small enclosed space. Druids and shamans, on the other hand, tend to work outdoors. The fact of large numbers of people celebrating with the same aim at the same times of the year raises a considerable amount of power from the group soul.

Samhain, also known as Hallowe'en, is the death of the old year and the rebirth of the new and thus can be said to be the start of the annual Pagan celebratory cycle. I will start my survey of the witches' year with this particular festival, which has been much misunderstood. For the Celts, the end of October was the time when, with the exception of the breeding stock, the remaining animals were slaughtered and salted down as they could not be fed through winter. This was an occasion for a celebration in which the tribespeople or villagers ate their fill before the lean times of winter. Far more importantly, this was the time of the year at which the veil between the living and the dead was almost transparent. Presiding over the feast was the Goddess in the aspect of the crone who guides us to the other world; Hecate, Morrigan, Cerridwen in her dark aspect are but a few of her names. The night belonged to neither past nor present and the division between this world and the next was seen as being briefly open. In Ireland it was believed that the fairy mounds, the dwellings of the *sidhe*, opened their doors and humans who desired could enter the realm of faerie. It was a time when the dead could return and gifted humans could divine the future in the leaping flames of the bonfire. In Celtic and Norse mythology, Samhain was the time of death for legendary kings and it may well have been the occasion for ritual human sacrifice, coupled with sexual rites to reaffirm the birth of the new year. In the Greek mysteries the Goddess descended to the underworld to dwell with the Dark Lord through the Winter before returning to bring forth new life in the Spring.

The element of sacrifice has been continued in the

British custom of celebrating Guy Fawkes' night on 5 November with bonfires, the burning of an effigy and fireworks. He tried to kill a king but, in his death, he became a ritual substitute. At around the same time of year as Samhain Hindus and Sikhs celebrate Diwali, which is a festival of light, with lamps in their homes, feasting and presents for their children. The Pagan urge to celebrate the onset of winter caused the Christian church to move the feast of the dead from May to the beginning of November. Thus the night of 31 October became the eve of All Hallows or All Souls Day and 2 November is celebrated as All Saints. In Catholic countries in Europe it is the custom to visit the family graves to decorate them with flowers and light lamps.

Hallowe'en is indelibly imprinted on non-Pagan minds as being associated with witchcraft, although many of its modern manifestations, such as children pestering their neighbours with demands for 'trick or treat', are trans-Atlantic imports. Pagan folk find it illogical that non-Pagans enjoy dressing up as witches, ghosts and devils and 'celebrating' the festival with fancy dress parties. Perhaps most of the population is Pagan at heart. Janet and Stewart Farrar have two celebrations — one the Samhain ritual for their coven and the other for the coven members, children and friends. According to the Farrars, 'children expect some fun out of Hallowe'en, and so (we have discovered) do friends and neighbours expect something of witches at Hallowe'en. So we hold a party and give it to them — pumpkins, masks, fancy-dress, leg-pulls, music, forfeits, local traditions — the lot.' One of the best such parties I have attended was given by a witch couple, slightly tongue in cheek, for their friends and neighbours at which an effigy of Mrs Thatcher was ceremonially burnt in the back garden. Paradoxically, fundamentalist Christians are greatly exercised about such innocent fun and in 1991 even managed to persuade Gwent Education Authority to ban Hallowe'en celebrations in their schools. Every year the newspapers are full of dire warnings about the supposed dangers to children from devilish practices that might lead them into the clutches of Satan.

In the ritual devised by the Farrars the altar is decorated with seasonal vegetation, nuts and fruit. The cauldron is placed in the centre of the circle with glowing charcoal on which after the opening invocation, the High Priestess scatters incense. The coven gather in a circle around the cauldron and, as the smoke rises, make silent communion with their loved ones who have passed on. This has nothing to do with spiritualism, as the dead are not invoked to appear, but rather it is a moment for quiet remembrance. The ritual finishes with the Great Rite being celebrated between the High Priest and Priestess as Samhain is regarded as a reaffirmation of life.

Ly Warren-Clarke, whose rituals are essentially for a witch working alone, regards Samhain as a time for looking into a mirror to divine the Ancient Wisdom. Traditionally that night is a time for divination and many witches who are natural clairvoyants feel introspective and withdrawn at Samhain. Another theme expressed in some published rituals is that of saying farewell to the summer goddess as she departs for the sleep of winter and to invoke her to appear again at spring.

After Samhain comes Yule, the festival of the Winter Solstice and the longest night. Yule literally means 'wheel', when the sun is at its lowest ebb but is reborn to regenerate its powers to nourish the earth in spring. It is at Yule that in so many traditions the goddess brings forth a boy child who will grow up to become both the Sun God and her lover-consort. Yule marks the death of the Old God, who impregnated the Goddess and is the father of the son who in turn will reimpregnate his mother-bride in the Spring. The miraculous births of Mithras, Osiris and the Welsh Pryderi, son of Rhiannon, all occurred at the time of the Winter Solstice. The death and rebirth of Dionysus was celebrated at Athens and the same theme can be found in the Indian legends surrounding Shiva. There is no hard and fast evidence as to when Jesus of Nazareth was born but it would seem to have been in the spring. It was in the year 273 that the church fixed the birth of Jesus at midwinter simply to bring him into line with the other Pagan sun gods as the child of a miraculously impregnated virgin goddess.

Yule symbolism is bound up with the light which is rekindled. In Sweden, 14 December sees the celebration of the festival of Saint Lucia in which a young girl, robed in pure white and wearing a crown of lighted candles on her head, processes from room to room escorted by her maidens. In Britain there is the tradition of the Yule log which should burn until 6 January, Twelfth Night, after which the ashes should be scattered on the land. The mistletoe, a plant sacred to the Druids, has retained its mystic link, as has the custom of decorating houses with evergreens and bringing in the Christmas tree.

Pagan ritual centres around the ceremonial lighting of a candle to signify the rebirth of the sun or, if working outside, the kindling of a fire. The working area is decorated with greenery and there will be food and drink prepared for the merrymaking afterwards. Yule is also the time when Pagans give personal presents to their loved ones and friends rather than waiting for Christmas which has no meaning for them. In the ritual devised by the Farrars an element of role playing or sacred drama is used to emphasize the message of the death and rebirth of the sun through figures they call the Oak King and Holly King. The Greeks made extensive use of drama to illustrate religious themes and the mystery plays of medieval Britain served the same purpose. The Holly King represents the god of the waning year and the Oak King the god of the coming one.

'Now, at the depth of winter, is the waning of the year accomplished, and the reign of the Holly King is ended. The sun is reborn, and the waxing of the year begins. The Oak King must slay his brother the Holly King and rule over my land until the height of summer, when his brother shall rise again.'

The actors playing the parts of the two kings then engage in symbolic combat and the Holly King falls to the ground where he is blindfolded. If well enacted in front of a large gathering, such plays can have a dramatic impact.

The first of the spring festivals is on 2 February, known to the Celts as Imbolc and Christianized as Candlemas. It also became the festival of Saint Brigid, who was derived from the Celtic Goddess Brid or Bride and was taken over by the new religion in an attempt to win Pagan hearts and minds. She is traditionally associated with sacred wells and there is a Bridewell in the City of London which is also the site of an old prison. The essence of the festival is the celebration of the stirrings of spring after the long winter darkness. This is the time when the Dark Lord releases the goddess from the underworld and allows her to return as a maiden to the earth to bring forth life again. On a different theme, the child born at Yule reaches puberty and begins to feel the stirring of his manhood as he is released from the care of his mother and must go out into the world. Jesus was presented to the rabbis in the Temple at this time, and for youthful Pagans it would also be a suitable occasion for making their own commitment to follow the Old Religion. February was also the traditional time of ritual purification, from which our custom of spring cleaning probably derives.

The theme of rebirth has made Imbolc a popular time for the performance of initiation ceremonies by Wiccan covens as it marks a starting point in the journey into the light. Ly Warren-Clarke, writing primarily for female witches, goes so far as to use ritual to enable the participant to undergo a visualized defloration, to signify her entry into womanhood. Candles again play a large part in the various Pagan observance and the Druids honour the Goddess with eight placed in a bowl of water. The Farrar ritual, a ceremonial representation of the Triple Goddess theme, is beautiful and moving although somewhat muddled in its symbolism. The maiden goes naked, holding a bunch of spring flowers and counterbalanced by the crone in a long dark cloak with her face hidden by a hood. Between them stands the Mother figure with a crown of lights which has been borrowed from Saint Lucia. Sadly, the Farrars recommend the construction of the device using torch bulbs and a hidden battery. This protects the High Priestess from singed hair but seems rather clinical for a Pagan celebration.

The second of the spring festivals is the equinox on 21 March when day and night are equal. At this point in his yearly evolution the god is poised between his subconscious animalism and the awareness of his conscious being. In myth he is the Stag Lord of the Forest, Herne the Hunter, still roaming free of responsibilities and taking his pleasures where he finds them. He will encounter the Goddess, symbolizing the *anima* or feminine within himself, and through their mating his successor will be conceived in the womb of the maiden. Spring is all about fertility for every living thing. Pagans, who are unashamed about sexuality, celebrate this most natural urge in song and ritual as their ancestors have done through the centuries. It is also the time of the Christian Easter, in itself a corruption of the name of the Nordic goddess Eostre, with its 'Easter bunnies' (notable for their fecundity) and chocolate eggs. In the more northerly countries, however, the ritual mating took place at Beltain owing to the much later arrival of spring.

The myth of the willing sacrifice of the god king and his eventual resurrection is parallelled in the story of the execution of Jesus of Nazareth who apparently went willingly and knowingly to his death, only to be resurrected. An earlier version of the same theme was based on the legend of the Phrygian Goddess Cybele whose son-lover Attis castrated himself, died and was reborn. In Egypt the spring rites were known as Behdet and celebrated the sacred marriage between the Goddess Hathor and the God Horus, coupled with the flooding of the Nile to bring fertility to the crops.

Pagans in Britain are divided as to whether the symbolic sacred marriage should be celebrated at the Equinox or Beltain, their views often depending on whether they accept the influence of Mediterranean culture or try to restrict themselves to more northern customs. Of overriding importance, however, is the emphasis on fertility, marked ritually by sowing seeds which can later be transplanted into the garden or a suitable wild place. Another custom used by some covens is the selection of a young female member as the Spring Queen who is then honoured in her aspect of the maiden goddess.

Beltain or May Eve is one of the most important dates for Pagans in Britain and is the traditional time for marriages, or 'handfastings' as they are called by witches. This was the time for Maypoles, dancing and the bringing of greenery into the churches, all of which echoed the Pagan past. In the evening the young men and maidens of the villages went 'a Maying', stealing off into the woods to do their bit for fertility. In the chapter on Pagan attitudes to sex there is a detailed discussion of sacred marriage, which forms an integral part of Beltain ritual whether actual or in token. Writers on witchcraft always stress that a sacred marriage should not be consummated in front of the coven, although some groups will undoubtedly disagree. Providing the couple concerned willingly volunteer there is no reason, except that of modern sensibilities, why others should be excluded.

Another ancient tradition observed by Pagans is the lighting of the Bel-fire which, in the case of a coven working indoors, consists of a candle in the cauldron. In the distant past tribespeople danced around the fire and then jumped over the glowing embers to ensure luck and fertility in the coming year.

On May Eve a traveller through the modern British countryside will perhaps see the odd fire burning in the darkness as small groups of Pagans gather in a quiet spot to celebrate the old rites. Lit by the flames, a young priestess garlanded with spring flowers may step forward to be ritually disrobed. As the worshippers link hands she leads them in the dance, weaving around the fire before being laid gently upon the ground. There, as has been the custom since time immemorial, she merges with the earth as her body is consecrated to form the altar. Then, as his presence is invoked, the God will stride into the light of the fire from the darkness of the surrounding woods to claim his bride. Laying his sword before her and shedding his cloak to reveal his manhood, the Horned One will be joined to the Goddess to bring fertility to all around them.

The Midsummer Solstice has been marred of late by scenes of violence at and around the Stonehenge site, which is discussed at some length in the final chapter. Stonehenge, an ancient sun temple, is closely associated with robed Druids performing their ceremony at sunrise. It is the time when the sun is at its greatest power, warming and fertilizing the crops, while the Goddess, blossoming in her pregnancy, pours out her love upon the Earth. In the year's cycle Midsummer marks the end of the reign of the Oak King who dies and gives way to the Holly King. The tradition of midsummer sacrifice and the spilling of blood in connection with fertility is discussed at great length by such anthropologists as Fraser and Margaret Murray.

The Druids hold an all-night vigil before the Solstice and their main ceremony at dawn. Those Pagans who have no desire to confront the might of the Wiltshire Constabulary take themselves out into the countryside to camp, make a fire and wait for the mystic rising of the Sun, imagining it perhaps appearing framed by a giant stone trilithon. For those who prefer to work skyclad, Midsummer is one of the few times of the year when this is comfortably possible in Britain, and some Wiccan covens have the use of private land where they can celebrate, dance and make merry.

Lugnasadh is the time of the year when the harvest begins and the grain is ready for cutting in the fields. Lugh was a Celtic corn deity of possibly Irish origin who was worshipped throughout the Bristish Isles. The Saxons referred to the festival as hlaf-mass or loaf mass, a reference to the grain harvest, and the Christians called it Lammas. Its fertility theme is likened by some

Pagans to the womb of the goddess pouring forth the bounty of nature for humans to enjoy and to store for the winter ahead. In some cultures the corn deity was sacrificed, cut down with the last sheaf of corn to rise again in the spring at the time of sowing. In some areas a flaming wheel was rolled down a hill to symbolize the transition from Summer to Autumn. In Pagan rituals at this time of year the working area is decorated with the fruits of the harvest and a home-made loaf of bread is often eaten in the circle. It also provides another chance to work outdoors, if a suitable site is available, where those taking part can perform the corn dance and afterwards feast in celebration of the harvest.

The Autumn Equinox is a second time of equilibrium and also a time of rest when the last of the harvest has been gathered. Now that the labour of summer has been completed, we prepare ourselves subconsciously for the winter months which lie ahead. The goddess is in the fullness of her pregnancy, while in the Greek myths she must depart for her sojourn in the Underworld, leaving the Earth in darkness. Many groups choose this time of the year to perform the legend of the descent of Persephone into Hades, where she is confronted by the image of Death in the person of the Dark God with whom she must come to terms. Thus the wheel of the Pagan year has turned full circle to bring us back to Samhain and the beginning of a new cycle.

Murry Hope, a qualified psychologist and occultist, has made a deep study of ritual observance and its power to satisfy basic human needs. In *The Psychology of Ritual* she wrote:

'Many of the peoples of earlier races and times possessed a more accurate concept of mankind's true role on earth than we have today in that they had an instinctive understanding of the ecological nature of things and the part they needed to play in order to maintain that delicate balance. The 'exchange of energies' concept has existed in both magic and religion since the dawn of time. People gave of what they had to the gods, nature entities, ancestral spirits and celestial deities in exchange for their bounty, the nature of which, although not fully understood by all, was considered a necessary prerequisite for the functioning of a balanced social and religious life. Failure to comply with this natural state of equipoise was guaranteed to bring down the wrath of the deities concerned.'

The concept of sacrifice in a physical sense is foreign to today's Pagans and witches who believe that the gods do not require the slaughter of animals and prefer the purity of intention of the celebrants who give of themselves rather than their goods. As Murry Hope explains, however, the basic principle of exchange still applies.

'Translated into a modern setting this could be seen to relate to the chaos which has resulted through mankind's misuse of nature's many bounties: "deforestation", dust bowls, the problem of nuclear waste, exploitation of natural resources and so on. As though the eco-related aspect of the human psyche is being awakened from its sleep or being re-educated following a period of regression, instinctive rites are slowly resurfacing from the collective inconscious in the form of a resurgence of old beliefs and religions which accommodate the Exchange of Energy Principle, that is, that one must always give in order to receive.'

This is a powerful rationale for the revival of Pagan beliefs in the modern world and explains in academic terms what an increasing number of people are discovering for themselves, whether in the drawing room or on a lonely hillside in the light of the Moon. This applies only to practising Pagans who have adopted ancient beliefs as part of their normal lives. There are, however, other rituals which awaken the same response deep in the psyche of individuals who are probably unaware of the significance of the experience they are undergoing. Murry Hope illustrates the effect of an ancient survival when describing the 'Obby Oss' festival at Padstow in Cornwall which, superficially, can be regarded as simple folklore. The festival is a publicly celebrated Spring rite, probably of Celtic origin, which every year draws large crowds to Padstow. She explains that it is far more than a seasonal fertility ritual, 'as it also serves to programme the subconscious and its somatic resonances to adapt to the ensuing weather conditions or elemental qualities that will dominate the oncoming cycle'.

The conduct of the ritual has probably been corrupted over the centuries, but it nevertheless retains the power to move all those taking part, whether throwing themselves heart and soul into the rite or purely there to see the fun. 'I was able to observe at first hand the effect of the constant drum beat and repetitive chanting . . . Evidence of the surfacing of some archaic Group Soul was abundantly clear to the experienced observer, the energies emitted reaching far deeper into the unconscious than the generally assumed fertility connotations.' Murry Hope is not a witch, but what she describes goes a long way towards explaining why it is that the seasonal festivals, wherever they are celebrated and whatever ritual is used, have a deep psychological impact on those who take part in them.

Vivienne Crowley is also a psychologist and happens to be a highly respected Wiccan High Priestess. She has written that anthropologists tend to see the seasonal celebrations of Pagans as being simply imitations of nature, but then asks why they needed to do that in the first place when nature was all around them. 'What they did need to express was not the outer world, which was there outside the door of the hut, but the inner world of the psyche, the interior drama arising from the unconscious in dreams and vision.'

It is here that Pagan observance differs from the mainstream religions and where much of its appeal lies for modern thinking folk. In many Christian churches the individual is purely an onlooker who obeys the rules while the priest or minister does what he has to do. The ancient Latin mass was a psychodrama of immense power and the Catholic church, by abandoning it, has lost much of its heritage. Witchcraft directly involves each coven member in the seasonal cycle enabling all to share in the unconscious linking with the past and the powers of Nature.

Vivienne Crowley, quoting from Karl Jung, argues that the inner reality portrayed in ritual, and the method of portrayal itself, used allegories found in Nature, 'for it was in part through observation of the cycle of birth, death, and rebirth in nature that human beings understood that this too was their own fate — to be born, to die and to live again'.

❧ 9 ❧
Witchcraft and Sex Magic

Sexual perversion is one of the most frequent accusations levelled against modern witches, both by the press and their detractors within the established religions. Even a whisper of the words sex and the occult is enough to trip a tabloid journalist's imagination into overdrive. However, by enforcing the belief that the only justification for the sexual act was procreation within wedlock, and in many cases banning contraception, the churches must shoulder much of the responsibility for the ills of present-day society. Pagans accept that there is no part of us that it not of the gods and, as the gods saw fit to equip us with sexual organs, they are there to be used without guilt. Christianity, on the other hand, has always advocated celibacy and virginity and failing that, abstinence. Even the misogynistic Saint Paul stated that it was better to marry than burn.

Paradoxically, the simultaneous waning of the influence of the churches and the sexual permissiveness of the 1960s did not add to the sum of human happiness. Promiscuity did not bring contentment but rather fuelled a rising tide of violence on our streets and the advent of sexually transmitted diseases. In spite of the acceptance of sex education and wide discussion of the subject in the media, crimes of violence against women are on the increase and teenage pregnancies are a source of great anxiety to those who have to provide for the mothers and their children.

Much of the blame must be laid at the door of the advertising profession which is devoted to the selling of sex as the desirable end-product of the purchase and consumption of consumer goods. Gender stereotyping ensures that a man is not a man unless he can sink interminable pints of lager and a woman is not a woman unless she attracts such a mate.

Pagans make no apologies for their views on sex and relations between the sexes, claiming that all levels of society can learn from the Craft, which is based on ancient beliefs but adapted to suit modern conditions. Witches have a healthy respect for sexuality and an ability to view it for what it is, the ultimate expression of love between a man and a woman and a celebration of the beautiful mystery of creation. Murry Hope succinctly wrote: 'To suppress the sexual function deliberately because of a guilt complex or moral confusion as to its correct use, is just as damaging to the psyche as the overuse of the faculty.'

Anyone who has read this far will have realized that much of Pagan worship is centred around fertility and that the symbolism used is essentially sexual. In the chapter on initiation into the Craft, I referred at some length to the sacred marriage, making the point that in the Wiccan tradition, where sex is used magically, it is a matter between two consenting adults who ideally are already established lovers. If an outsider chanced to come across a coven meeting in a woodland glade on the night of the full moon, he might well see a group of naked people dancing together in a circle. Ironically, the section of the media which condemns this as obscene also purveys nudity as a desirable commodity. It would be foolish to deny that orgies do take place under the umbrella of the occult, but they are indulged in by groups seeking thrills rather than spiritual enlightenment.

Christian philosophy divorces sex from the religious experience. Yet in many of the ancient religions sex was an integral part of worship and belief and operated at two levels: the public ceremonies that were more often than not an excuse for bawdy revelry; and rituals in the temples that were reserved for the initiated priesthood.

One of the very first principles discovered by primitive man was that sex was the key to survival, apart from being a delightful experience in itself. Cave paintings show the act of lovemaking and many artefacts that have survived are figurines which portray exaggerated genitals and pregnant females. In a tribal grouping, a woman who was particularly fruitful and bore many sons became a person of respect, the archetype perhaps of the Mother Goddess figure. Among the men the best hunter gained the most respect and thus the first choice of the available females, in the belief that his genes in the offspring would provide further good hunters. As society became more organized, the basic religious impulse was codified and a priesthood developed from among those members of the group who showed an aptitude for interceding with the Gods on behalf of the others. At the same time the skilled hunter became elevated to the status of ruler or king and his virility became bound up with the fertility of the people as a whole. As his sexual powers waned, so he had to be sacrificed and replaced by a younger and stronger man who would have to prove his virility by mating publicly with a specially chosen female. The sceptre as the symbol of kingship is after all, only a representation of the erect penis — an upright staff with a knob on the end.

In this ritual lie the origins of the sacred marriage which in turn is the basis of sex magic and is echoed in religious traditions throughout the world. Even in the Middle Ages in Christian Europe a royal wedding was consummated in front of witnesses and often the bride had to prove her virginity. The ruler had to have a son to succeed him to keep his family clan in power. If he failed, he was no longer sacrificed but his prestige inevitably waned. The wedding ceremony is still shot through with Pagan symbolism. The bride is dressed in white and veiled, the symbol of the neophyte prepared for initiation, and she is attended by maids. Before the altar she is 'joined' in holy matrimony to the bridegroom in celebration of the divine polarity. In the words of the *Book of Common Prayer* the partners vow, 'with my body I thee worship'. At the reception they effect the communion with champagne and the cutting of the cake, often with a borrowed sword. The rice and confetti that are thrown on their departure are fertility symbols as they head off to consummate their union, without which the ceremony is null and void.

The act of sexual union is at the heart of many of the myths and legends which have come down to us from the past. The Greek gods were a randy lot with a great taste for mortal women with whom they conceived a legion of demi-gods and goddesses. Considerable sections of the *Old Testament* are devoted to begetting and as a boy I was fascinated by looking up the 'naughty bits'. Then I discovered *The Golden Bough*, which had enough about sex in it to satisfy the curiosity of the most prurient teenager, at a time when girlie magazines were unheard of. Sacred sculpture and painting in the past saw no reason to disguise the facts of life and openly portrayed male gods with erect penis and couples joined in the most acrobatic of embraces. Erotic frescoes were to be found in many ordinary Greek and Roman houses, as fertility and hence the sexual act were part and parcel of religious belief. There was no need to invent euphemisms about sex in societies which saw nothing shameful or indecent about sexuality.

Today we live among a riot of phallic symbols: tall office blocks, sports cars, the lollipop-shaped microphones fondled by pop singers, even sticks of rhubarb. Yet such are the indecency laws that sexual symbolism has to be delivered to the subconscious and what can be shown or not shown is governed by regulation. In the ancient world climate combined with lack of inhibition to make nudity an accepted fact of life. The Greeks had a merry little god called Priapus, and statues of him sporting an enormous erection were set up in gardens, orchards and fishing ports to ensure fertility. Many modern travellers to Greece bring back a small plaster statuette of Priapus in their luggage, but definitely not for the mantelpiece when the vicar comes to tea. The Egyptian god, Min, was a similar deity, always portrayed erect. The traditional barber's pole is a direct descendant of the signs displayed outside shops in the ancient world to bring prosperity. Greek market places featured a pillar in the shape of a penis dedicated to Hermes.

In India sacred sculpture featured the yoni, or vulva, and the lingam or penis as objects of worship. Temples were decorated with intricate carvings of every possible position for sexual intercourse with no attempt made to screen them from public view. Chinese and Japanese art

165

abounds with delicate but explicit paintings of men and women making love, attended perhaps by some musicians and servants offering food. In Greece athletes competed naked as a matter of course. One could argue that this custom should be reintroduced, to abolish the problem of competitors being used as running and jumping billboards by advertisers keen to emphasize the number of stripes on their shoes. In many cultures temple prostitution was an institution; in Babylon every woman once in her life had to serve any man who wanted her at the temple of the Goddess Mylitta.

These customs can be dismissed as examples of decadent societies and pious writers have often argued that reason for their decline lay in their moral depravity. Leaving aside the public bawdiness of the classical world, what was it that went on in the secret ceremonies in the temples? Few details of these ceremonies survived but they certainly involved sexual intercourse designed to celebrate the divine mystery — the union of the male and female principle. In the Eleusinian Mysteries in Greece, for example, the object was to enable the initiate to attain knowledge of the divine spark within.

Some mystical traditions claim that this state is to be achieved through mental discipline, prayer, meditation and asceticism. Other schools, notably those in the East, have always favoured divine attainment through sex on the basis that it is first necessary to experience the darker side of nature before the divine can be attained. The basis of our knowledge of Eastern sex magic is to be found in a body of ancient Hindu and Buddhist texts known as the Tantra, many of which were translated during the Victorian era and privately published for a limited readership.

To understand the spiritual application of Eastern

eroticism a number of concepts need explanation and a working knowledge of yoga is useful. Indian adepts see the human body as having seven centres of vital energy, which they call the *chakras*, the lowest of which is situated at the base of the spine or genital area. They then run up the body via the stomach, solar plexus, heart, throat, forehead or third eye position to the crown of the head. The *chakras* are used by many Pagans as a method of drawing energy, or *prana*, into the body as a meditative exercise; any good book on yoga will tell you how to do it. The technique is to draw in energy through the base of spine *chakra* so that it rises up the other *chakras*, diffusing through the whole body in the process. The visualization is of a serpent known as Kundalini which lies curled at the base of the spine and when awakened can be made to rise up the spinal column.

It is important not to confuse Tantric worship with the satisfaction of base desires. In the words of Murry Hope: 'If, however, the sexually orientated rite is used purely for self-indulgence and titillation, then intention decrees the level of the energies that will be attracted, and the Kundalini or serpent power of the participants will proceed no further than the lower *chakras*, which are liable to become effectively blocked.'

Tantric worship centres on the God Shiva and the Goddess Shakti and the aim is to identify with these archetypes by means of ritual. Any lustful thoughts in the minds of the participants will not only vitiate the discipline but could also court psychic danger. Tantra involves a high degree of mental preparation. This can involve meditation on a symbolic diagram known as a *yantra*, the learning of breathing techniques to control orgasm and the chanting of sacred mantras.

A Tantric ritual can be worked with a group, as would

have been the custom in India, or between a couple. In the former the participants sat in a circle, alternating between men and women, under the direction of a leader and worshipped the naked body of a priestess in the centre. One of the keys to the ceremony was a ritual meal based on the principle of the four elements and spirit (pentagram). Wine equated to fire, meat to air, fish to water, grain to earth and sexual intercourse to spirit. There are Tantric groups in existence today, but in the West it is difficult to assemble a group of participants who have reached the mental level necessary to perform the rituals.

The following is an example involving a couple who have studied the images and legends of Shiva and Shakti and believe that they have the ability and dedication for the rituals, and without which they should not comtemplate the attempt.

They will need a clear space of floor covered with plenty of blankets and cushions and a small table on which the ritual meal is spread — some wine and meat, fish and grain dishes. If they propose to work for a specific purpose they need to fix the intention firmly in their minds and consider colour symbolism in their choice of robes, flowers, table covering, the food and the incense. When everything is prepared they must bathe carefully and put on clean robes that are easily removable from above without having to be peeled over the head. On entering the temple they must sit in meditation for a while to centre themselves and then enjoy the meal together, feeding each other and talking quietly. Nothing at any stage must be hurried and the full ritual should last several hours.

Having eaten, the worship starts as Shiva and Shakti lovingly caress each other while still robed, visualizing themselves as the God and Goddess, and then lower their robes to the waist. The caressing continues, avoiding the genital areas, until both are naked, at which point Shakti lies in the centre of the circle. Shiva sits silently contemplating her and worshipping her as the Goddess she has become, drawing in energy through his base-of-spine *chakra* and projecting it into her as glowing light. When he feels ready he changes places with her and she in turn worships and energizes him. Only then does she begin slowly and gently to stimulate him sexually, rubbing him with perfumed oil and using her tongue. Once again they change places and Shiva takes up the love play until Shakti's yoni is ready. The classic position for their union is for Shiva to sit in the lotus position and for Shakti to sit on him with her arms locked around his body. Few Westerners can manage this and it is best if Shiva either sits with his legs out in front or lies on his back.

Shakti lowers herself onto him as lingam and yoni unite and they embrace tightly, slowing down and synchronizing their breathing, becoming one in the sacred marriage of God and Goddess. Shakti is the one who moves, making only enough effort to maintain Shiva's erection. They must sense the serpent power rising through their bodies by slow stages to reach the crowns of their heads when the marriage reaches its final consummation in the orgasmic moment of the divine light.

Similar rituals were the basis of the secret worship in the ancient temples where coming to terms with physical desire was regarded as a prerequisite to attaining the ultimate spiritual knowledge. This is reflected in the Wiccan Great Rite which can achieve the same effect if those performing it are sufficiently trained to know what they are doing. As lust is entirely divorced from the proceedings, the Great Rite can in theory be carried out as a ritual act between any man and woman without exciting the jealousy of their respective partners.

The same secret knowledge, derived from Mediterranean rather than Eastern sources, was driven underground at the beginning of the Christian era, thereafter resurfacing only in discreetly coded forms. There has been much speculation about the reasons the Church found to eradicate the Knights Templar with such ruthlessness. The ostensible reason was the Knights' wealth, which was coveted by the Pope and the King of France, but there were the charges of diabolism. The Knights certainly had come into contact with Eastern mystic ideas during the Crusades and there is evidence that they possessed the ancient secrets.

It is the author's belief that although the Knights Templar were using occult knowledge, it is unlikely that sex magic featured in their practices as they were an all male order. If sex was involved it was probably *per anem*, which can generate a high degree of energy but, by breaking the basic law of polarity, cannot achieve the ultimate goal of union with the divine.

Another clue to the puzzle is provided by the writings of the alchemists which in turn can be linked with the various Rosicrucian orders which flourished in the seventeenth and eighteenth centuries. At one level, Alchemy was a pseudo-science devoted to transmuting base metals into gold. But the alchemists' quest for the Philosopher's Stone and the Elixir of Life brings us back full circle to Aleister Crowley, who is the key to understanding Wiccan use of sex in ritual. Crowley decoded the alchemical symbolism but continued to use the terms to keep the secret within the circle of high adepts. He likened the *athanor*, or furnace, to the male sexual organs in which the 'first matter' or sperm, known as the Blood of the Red Lion, was generated. The *cucurbite*, or retort, was the female vagina which when excited is lubricated by the fluid that was disguised as the Gluten of the White Eagle. The mingling of the two fluids during intercourse was transmuted by the wills of the participants into the Elixir which was then consumed as the eucharist. Crowley refers enigmatically to this communion in an essay entitled *Of the Eucharist and of the Art of Alchemy*, published in his book *Magick in Theory and Practice*. Consuming the consecrated elements also featured in Tantric ritual, and it is probable that Crowley gained the knowledge from his study of ancient sources.

Whatever one may think of Crowley as a person, there is no doubt that he was a high adept as far as the practice of magic was concerned. Sex lies at the core of much of his vast output and was taught to his pupils, although in his published works the secrets remained. One of Crowley's pupils was Israel Regardie, who included in his book, *The Tree of Life*, a chapter on a rite he called The Mass of the Holy Ghost. This was first published in 1932 in the United States where the prevailing moral climate would probably have resulted in a spell in prison for the author had he been explicit. Regardie begins by stating that his purpose in writing the book is to describe all magical processes lucidly and simply without resorting to the deliberate deceptions which were often inserted into earlier works. However, 'there remains to be outlined in this work one secret formula of practical Magic of such a tremendous nature – shrouded as it always has been in the past by the glamour of recondite symbols and hidden by heavy veils – that the writer is doubtful as to whether it would be wise or politic to adhere to his original decision. If carefully studied the terms employed will reveal a consistency and a continuity which will disclose to the right people in a quite accurate manner the processes of its techniques.'

He continues, in extremely flowery prose, to describe the secret ritual of the alchemists whereby a living substance is transmuted into a powerful talisman, in the Holy Grail itself. The Grail, or chalice of the communion in his Mass, is the vagina of the officiating priestess into which is poured *Amrita*, the dew of immortality, the weapons used being the cup and the wand. Regardie may have been purposely obscure but he makes the vital point most eloquently.

'The supreme power operating in this technique is love. Trite though it may seem, and hackneyed though the work itself has become, it must be reiterated that love is the motivating power; a love force held always in leash by the Will and controlled by the Soul. The destructive power of the Sword and all that the Sword implies, the dispersive character of the dagger or any of the other elemental weapons, has no place herein. This method therefore commends itself as being of the very highest. Since it does partake of love, it is of the stuff and essence of life itself.'

Regardie does not give a set ritual formula but recommends invocation of the divine force required as the Blood of the Red Dragon is heated slowly in the furnace, which must only be discharged into the chalice when it has reached white heat. The process of heating should be accompanied by a short rhythmically repeated mantra to fix the intent firmly in the linked minds of the participants. The completion of the mass is the communion whereby the sacred elements are consumed directly from the chalice, which Crowley recommended should be by means of thumb and forefinger, care being taken not to spill any. The elements can also be used to consecrate sacred weapons and to empower talismans with the vital life force created by the intention of the priest and priestess.

So there it was at last, in black and white, in a published book and available to anyone who could understand the symbolism. One could argue, though, that similar codes have been used by poets through the ages. The lady was often likened to a blood-red rose full of sweet nectar by the poet, who longed to meet her in her perfumed garden or in her rose-girt bower. The code can be seen in secret hidden valley of desire, or in Shakespeare's words, 'where the bee sucks, there suck I'. Such erotic imagery, which had been part and parcel of the language of love from classical times, reappeared in southern Europe at the time of the troubadours – the romantic poets and singers of the early Middle Ages.

We have seen in the chapter on the revival of the Craft in Britain that Gerald Gardner was involved via Aleister Crowley in the O.T.O. (Ordo Templo Orientalis). Organised on lines similar to Freemasonry, the Order had a number of degrees, of which the lower ones were purely instructional. When Crowley founded the British branch he translated and rewrote the degrees to conform to his own ideas. The eighth degree is concerned with auto-sexual acts and recommends masturbation for the purposes of raising the necessary sexual energy and producing a 'living substance', although that might well be self defeating as it would lack the essential polarity. It may well be the origin, however, of Crowley's boast that he had sacrificed 150,000 babies, although to achieve that total he must have spent an inordinate amount of time in masturbation. In his eleventh degree intercourse *per anem* is considered, which certainly reflected the Beast's own proclivities.

The origin of the Wiccan Great Rite is to be found in the ninth degree of the O.T.O. which involves intercourse between a priest and priestess followed by consumption of the generated fluids. Doreen Valiente states that this was the practice in the Gardner coven, although without the communion, but always in private between the couple concerned. Much of the wording of this ceremony and the ritual gestures were taken wholesale from Crowley's beautifully worded and majestic Gnostic Mass. In addition to being the central pillar of the Third Degree initiation, Gardner specified that the Great Rite should be performed at each of the Sabbats by the officiating priest and priestess but without the rest of the coven being present. This tradition is perpetuated in the seasonal rituals devised by the Farrars. One wonders what the rest of the coven do when they leave. Perhaps someone puts the kettle on for a quick cup of coffee while others use the time to go to relieve themselves or smoke a cigarette. A gaggle of naked people milling around in the corridor waiting for the priest and priestess to get on with it seems a slightly farcical notion. It also misses the point of the intrinsic intimacy required for working sex magic and the need to take time.

This kind of working is most effective when performed with a firm intention by a couple on their own. Janet and Stewart Farrar have written that they performed the Great Rite together shortly after moving to Ireland in order to attract like-minded people. Their intention was to raise an 'astral lighthouse' over their cottage which they projected at the climax of the ritual. As a result they met a couple who became their first initiates there. All sensible writers on the subject, including the Farrars, stress the absolute basis of love and worship needed for the performance of any such ritual, without which the energy will never rise above the purely genital level. From this it is clear that sex which is often used by practitioners of black magic is doomed to failure and may well cause severe damage to the participants.

In the past many books dealing with the religious

aspects of sex in antiquity, sheltered behind the author's moral disapproval while enjoying healthy sales. Until the publication of several works on Wicca in recent years, occult literature cloaked the obvious in symbolism and metaphor. However, *The Tree of Ecstasy*, an advanced manual of sex magic written by Dolores Ashcroft-Nowicki, a well-known ceremonial magician, and published in 1991, is the best contribution to the literature on the subject.

The author gives eleven rituals based around the symbolism of the Kabbalistic Tree of Life. In her introduction, she writes: 'Such rituals are also a very potent form of High Magic and not to be worked lightly. Neither are they to be demeaned by using them simply for the self-gratification of sexual intercourse and giving nothing to the Gods. To do so will be to invite upon yourselves a swift and exacting retribution, for you do not use the creative force of the cosmos under ritual conditions for your own human lust. The dedication and concentration of purpose is what sets these rituals apart from anything you may have been told or have read about in the past.'

Ashcroft-Nowicki's scheme presupposes an established couple working the rituals who have at least some knowledge of basic magical principles and the necessary dedication to prepare thoroughly for each one. The preparations vary but involve physical exercises based on yoga and meditation upon the individual themes. One ritual per month is laid down as the maximum, owing to their intensity and the necessity for proper preparation which also includes periods of celibacy before a working. The author stresses the overriding need for purity of both body and mind before undertaking such rituals. 'Just as every man is a priest of love, so every woman becomes "the Royal High Priestess", the chalice that uplifts, accepts and enroyals her priest, transmuting the seed of life either into a new human being or into an offering of love to the Creator.'

Each ritual, besides being based on the ascending spheres of the Tree, has a different theme and thus God forms. The first is a rite of Pan, that most earthy and lustful of Gods, and is designed to start the ascent of the couple into higher realms. Each one has an important lesson to teach about the essence of love and how this has traditionally been expressed in legend and myth. Particularly emotive is a celebration of the sacred marriage, called the Grail of Grace, and placed in the sphere of Chesed on the tree of life. Chesed represents the number four and is associated with maturity and responsibility, signifying that the couple are ready to take on a firm spiritual commitment to each other. The couple who are going to work the ritual need another couple to act as priest and priestess for the first part, which is ceremonial, but they leave before the actual consummation.

Another of the rituals, entitled the Calling of a Soul, is dedicated to the conception of a child by the couple. The author writes: '. . . to invoke a special soul to indwell the body ritually prepared for it is to attempt one of the highest and most heart-rendingly beautiful of all rituals.' Those are the words of an accomplished occultist and she goes on to say; 'To conceive a child is to accept responsibility for another life, a life that may be important to the world in the future, or maybe a life that will one day set off a chain of circumstances that will change history, or it may simply be a life that will offer love and the promise of your family's immortality through its bloodline.' This is an excellent summary of Pagan attitudes to the conception of children and a corrective to the public's prurient obsession with alleged sexual perversion.

At this stage the reader has two options. The first is to dismiss the concept of sex coupled with religion as being both depraved and 'dirty' and to condemn all witches as perverts. The second is to take a hard look at one's own sexuality, and that of one's partner, and to consider whether Pagan philosophy has a positive contribution to society. Judaeo-Christian moral restrictions have become so firmly anchored in people's subconscious that any expression of sexuality is outwardly frowned upon while guilt is assuaged by prurient sniggering. Pagans prefer sex without shame rather than obtaining it second-hand.

Many Pagans hope that the coming of the Aquarian Age will bring a more enlightened view of human sexuality, enabling both men and women to see each other as equals rather than as sexes in a state of perpetual war. Put crudely but with feeling, Pagans hope that, one day, Mary will be able to remove her robe and cast off her virginity, and that Jesus will be able to drop his loincloth, so that the worshippers will be able to finally recognize them for what they are — the eternal Goddess and her lover/son, the Lord of Creation.

❦ 10 ❦
The Age of
Aquarius

There are a number of possible reactions to the subject matter of the book, having read thus far. One is that the reader will remain convinced that anything to do with the occult is intrinsically evil and that anyone who dabbles in it will come to a sticky end. Another predictable reaction is that it is all slightly dotty and certainly ridiculous. A third possibility is that the reader may feel that Witchcraft or Paganism of some sort appeals to his or her ideals and is worthy of further consideration. The fact that such activities exist and are on the increase, can be simply dismissed out of hand, giggled about or accepted, according to the individual viewpoint. The purpose of the book has not been to win converts, but rather to explain what Paganism is about and how its practitioners see themselves. There has been scant mention of Satanism, as that particular form of activity has nothing to do with the subject matter of the book. This last chapter will be an attempt to provide an answer to the question as to whether Paganism has something to offer society in the future or will it remain a cult on the loony fringe? It is a fact that interest in Wicca and all the other variants that make up the Pagan spectrum is on the increase at the moment, fuelled by a veritable spate of books that are being published in ever increasing numbers. There seems to be a genuine hunger for new levels of personal spiritual experience at the dawning of the Aquarian Age, and the Pagan phenomena is directly parallelled in Christianity. People are fleeing in their droves from the sterility of experience in the mainstream denominations and embracing the intensity of movements such as the Pentecostals, the Charismatics and the Evangelicals.

The tragedy is that Pagans and the new Christians appear to be on a collision course. The recently proclaimed Decade of Evangelism has declared open season on the occult and hordes of earnest young people will be fanning out equipped with their banners and hymns to convert the unfortunate Pagans. The paradox is, of course, that Wicca and Paganism are non-evangelistic in their approach to belief and would not wish to ram their opinions down anyone's throat. I have certainly never suffered from the attentions of the local Pagans knocking at my door or stuffing tracts into my hands while shopping. I once asked a witch friend for her views on Christianity, and she replied; 'Oh, I'm not against it, I am just mystified by its intensity.' Thinking Pagans find it quite incomprehensible that people can still kill each other in the name of religion and that fanatisicm has engendered so many tribal conflicts — in Northern Ireland, the rump of what was Yugoslavia and the inter-sect feud between Sunni and Shia Muslims to name but a few.

The New Age that was born in the sixties is a label that has been attached to a whole variety of notions and people, and is so vast a concept that it is incapable of definition, but some would argue convincingly that Paganism is the religion of the New Age folk. Like many such generalisations there is a germ of truth in this, yet all the feelings of love, peace and harmony have been slow in coming to fruition. It must be stated though, that New Age interests are perfectly compatible with being a member of any religious denomination or branch of faith. One thing that is totally alien to New Age thinking, however, is fanaticism, occupied as it is with the problems facing the environment and the whole of humanity rather than just a particular section.

The Age of Aquarius is a well used expression, but few know what it is and when it is due to start. In fact, it is all to do with a mixture of astronomy and astrology. As the earth moves in its orbit and rotates on its axis it shifts ever so slightly out of true over a period of 25,920 years. This is divided up into twelve 'months' corresponding to the signs of the Zodiac, each of which consists of around 2,000 earth years. Astrologers tell us that we are in the final phase of the Piscean Age and entering into the sign of Aquarius. So what, the sceptic may well say. Astrology is all a lot of rubbish anyway. But Pisces, the fish, is a water element and the last two thousand years roughly approximate to the Christian era. Pisceans have a tendency to be passive and swim with the tide, which is what a lot of mankind has been doing, content to swallow the dictates of the revealed religions. Aquarius on the other hand, is all about air, freedom, independence of thought and the concept of a brotherhood of man. Astrologers and magicians cannot come up with an exact date for the dawn of the reign of Aquarius but it is surely no accident that Aquarian thought patterns burst upon an unsuspecting world in the sixties.

David Conway, a ritual magician and extremely lucid writer whose book, *Secret Wisdom*, is by far and away the best summary of the intellectual background to magic, was scathing about this tentative dawn and I quote his comments at some length.

'It was in the 1960s, amidst the flower power, macrobiotic food, Zen Buddhism and endless talk of peace and love, that there appeared to be signs of an occult renaissance, with young people determined to make the transcendental a part of their everyday lives. There was, of course, nothing new in this; the novelty was only that with the widespread decline of religious belief this perennial yearning for the numinous could no longer be satisfied, as it had been in the past, by organised religion. As a result, large numbers turned to occultism in the hope of encountering the supernatural without any of the theological preconditions their intellect was not prepared to accept. In doing so, however, the majority soon left their intellect behind, blithely forgetting that all experience, be it of this world, or, more importantly, of other worlds, has always to be subject to critical appraisal. Instead these starry-eyed converts to occultism went their own happy, hippy way, accepting all they came across at its face value: flying saucers, horoscopes, ghosts, ghouls, Atlantis — all had their unthinking supporters, people who needed to believe in them as much as others needed to believe in the fairytale sagas of Professor Tolkien.'

That somewhat harsh judgement is in many ways well deserved and it is easy to poke fun at New Age people with their fads and their endless searching for meaning, all wrapped up in pseudo scientific language. One of the most delightful expose's of New Ageism is Martin Stott's book, *Spilling the Beans*, in which he coined the expression 'Alternative Types' or AT's to describe the subjects of his gentle satire. A glance through various fringe magazines will provide the reader with endless possibilities for self-improvement via meditation, crystal therapy, holistic massage, rebirthing, pyramid transformation, image work, sacred dance and psychosynthesis.

Nonetheless, it is possible to argue that David Conway got it wrong. From the lofty intellectual plane of the ceremonial magician it is easy to look down on the mass of ordinary folk struggling to find some meaning to their existence as the old order was stripped bare before their eyes. The passage to adulthood in the 1960s was a heady experience as a new generation listened to the songs of Bob Dylan and sympathised with the human rights campaigners. In 1968 the students rioted in Paris and brought down de Gaulle; the miniskirt came and went and the young started to worry about the environment. Yet the energy ran down as we entered the sterile seventies and was dispelled by the decade of the Yuppie. Anarchic Punk replaced songs about love and peace, listened to under a gentle haze of cannabis smoke. Yet underneath the veneer of greed that gripped society in the 1980s, Paganism flourished, attracting new adherents and redefining its philosophies.

In a previous chapter I alluded at some length to the importance of the Stonehenge festivals in the context of the Pagan revival. The subsequent history of the Stonehenge movement is a tragic one marred by violence and brutality, as the authorities combined to put a stop to the 'medieval brigands' who had no place in Thatcher's Britain. Yet at the time of writing, the so-called New Age travellers are still a regular news item. Many of them are undoubtedly a thorough pest to the public at large, but the travellers themselves feel that media opinion is stacked against them. It is therefore worthwhile to briefly consider what happened as the subject of the convoy is germane to any study of the continuation of Pagan thought.

The Rainbow travellers who were evicted from Molesworth wandered slowly south during the Spring of 1985 and finally congregated in Savernake Forest on land owned by the Earl of Cardigan. It was well known that the authorities intended to stop attempts to hold a festival that year but all concerned felt that they had a right to be there. On 1 June a convoy of battered vehicles formed up and moved off towards Stonehenge in beautiful weather with flags flying and everybody in a happy peaceful mood. 'It was an epic ride, the biggest and most magnificent convoy ever, stretching and snaking its way over the Wiltshire Downs ahead and behind as far as the eye could see. When we passed though villages people stood outside the doorways of their houses smiling and waving at us.'

Overhead, the police helicopter hovered and the head of the convoy found their way barred by a huge pile of gravel. They turned off into a smaller road which led them onto the main A303 near Cholderton. This was blocked by two huge lorries full of gravel and behind them the police were waiting. They began attacking the first vehicles, smashing windows and arresting those inside. These were the opening shots in what was to become known as the 'Battle of the Beanfield'.

The following vehicles moved off the road through the fence and into a field of beans escaping the violence at the roadblock. After a while a lull descended while the police brought up reinforcements. During the afternoon attempts were made to negotiate and the travellers agreed to leave peacefully and disperse. However, by the early evening it became clear that the police were preparing to charge. Panic broke out as engines were started and vehicles began to drive in circles to escape the mass of riot-equipped police, who were not easy-going Wiltshire bobbies but men hardened on the miners' picket lines.

'Half way up the field we noticed a woman clutching a baby running our way. We stopped and picked her up and set off again driving in circles like hunted prey. Other vehicles crossed the confusion and everything was spinning. The lady handed me her baby who can't have been more than nine months . . . Six officers with riot sticks surrounded the front of the coach and started smashing the front windows. Glass flew everywhere, I handed the baby back to her guardian and noticed one officer go round to the driver's window where Lin was still seated and smashed it with his stick, then the big window directly behind that where the baby slept oblivious.'

'Paraffin poured on children's beds; oil poured over the interiors of buses and caravans, in one case the contents of a chemical toilet; beds and furniture wrecked; guitars and other musical instruments smashed; money missing; personal effects ripped up (letters, paintings and photos); wiring ripped out; ignition keys missing; windows and interior panels smashed.'

The above are quotations from just two of those involved. The Earl of Cardigan said: 'I shall never forget the screams of one woman who was holding up her little baby in a bus with smashed windows. She screamed and screamed at them to stop but five seconds later fifty men with truncheons and shields just boiled into that bus. It was mayhem, no other word for it.'

Some 520 peaceful travellers were arrested and dispersed at police stations throughout the south of England. Peoples' homes had been wrecked and dozens had been injured by blows from truncheons, including pregnant women. A peaceful protest had been turned into a bloodbath. The survivors retreated to the Earl of Cardigan's woods to lick their wounds; the site was likened to a refugee camp as those released from prison straggled in over the following days. The Earl refused the police access to his land and thus gave the battered remnants of the Rainbow tribe a chance to repair as much of the damage as possible. Local people and other sympathizers rallied round with generous gifts of food, clothing and toys for the children, after harrowing scenes were shown on television.

In the long run the result of the police action proved counter-productive. It polarized opinion and attracted undesirable elements to the travellers. The following year there was another violent confrontation at Stoney Cross in the New Forest where the late John Duke, Chief Constable of Hampshire, vowed to 'decommission' the convoy. Hundreds were arrested, riot police wantonly smashed vehicles and lashed out with their truncheons. A large section of the press applauded the action taken against the 'hippy menace', which had the effect of encouraging lawless elements to attach themselves to the travellers in the hope of having a go at the police. In 1988, 5,000 people massed in Wiltshire near Stonehenge and were finally allowed on foot up to the stones, cordoned off by a massive police presence. Both sides subsequently accused each other of having started the trouble, but a riot broke out and the police charged the packed throng. Eerily lit by the searchlights of hovering helicopters, men, women and children fled in panic down the slopes and away from the stones. Lines of vans fitted wtih riot grilles patrolled the surrounding area and the protesters were gradually hemmed in and dispersed.

'The Banana Moon rose, closely followed by Venus, as

we linked hands to form a large circle. We prayed to our gods and goddesses and remembered those who had not made it this far. Those killed, like Wally Hope, those injured or in prison. We vowed to reach the stones for them. The Chalice was lit and passed slowly, formally, around the circle. Each person paused to contemplate as the communion ritual was performed. Finally we linked arms and danced three times sunwise around the tumulus, ending in a huge hug and a cheer in the middle . . .'

Since then the original Pagan element of the Stonehenge movement has stayed away, preferring to celebrate the Solstice in peace elsewhere or to stay at Glastonbury when there is a commercial festival. The access to the temple may have been banned, at vast cost to the ratepayers of Wiltshire, but the moving spirit has not been crushed. In spite of police action and the taint of violence, the true Pagans have gained in strength, and have been permitted to visit the stones at the less important festivals of the Winter Solstice and the Spring and Autumn Equinoxes. Relatively small numbers of Rainbow folk have arrived, been allowed in to the enclosure and have then left, without doing any damage and taking their litter with them.

Yet in spite of the harassment and the draconian application of the Public Order Act, the urge felt by a section of society to travel, and then to congregate at certain times of the year, remains strong. The travellers have had a strong influence on the spiritual development of New Age thinking as a whole, yet theirs has not been a lone voice. After its landmark fifteen per cent showing in the 1989 European Parliamentary elections, political support for the Green Party has fallen away, prompting many commentators to write the Greens off as a political force. Nevertheless the effect of the Greens'

1989 triumph was the increased greening of the mainstream political parties as they bowed to public opinion. Green views go hand in hand with Pagan views and some predict that Paganism will be the new religion of the environmentally conscious. People have woken up to the fact that global warming is not just scientific scaremongering and that the damage to the ozone layer seems to be drifting uncomfortably closer to home. Many folk are asking why the established religions seem to have so little to say about such issues which threaten all our futures.

Events at a local and international level suggest that a new decade is painfully adapting to new priorities. The police have been thrown on to the defensive after revelations of large-scale malpractice over many years and it is to be hoped that a new consensus will emerge on their future role. Mrs Thatcher has been cast into the political wilderness by her own party, leaving behind her the debris of the uncollectable Poll Tax which swept so many into the arms of the general protest movement. Authoritarian rule in the Soviet Union and the East European satellite states has crumbled from within and the first elected president of a free Czechoslovakia was a dissident playwright by the name of Vaclav Havel. The Samhain edition of *The Wiccan* contained news of approaches made to the Pagan Federation by groups in Lithuania and Latvia where, in spite of Communism, interest in the traditional culture and the Old Religion continued underground. Poland, that most Catholic of countries, so long starved of free access to information, seems to have embraced a flood of New Age ideas with enthusiasm, many of which have been imported from the United States.

It has become fashionable in the tabloid press to laugh at the Prince of Wales because he talks to his plants and to ridicule his interest in anything that could be remotely described as New Age, yet people with consciences look to him as a future leader. He has demonstrated that he is prepared to tilt at the bastions of the architectural establishment and has repeatedly demonstrated that he really cares.

There is also a refreshing wind blowing through the business world, entrenched as it is in greed and exploitation. Anita Roddick, the founder of the Body Shop chain, is another of the great hopes for the future and living proof that such terms as care and love are not the prerogative of a bunch of scruffy drop-outs dodging the police on Salisbury Plain. She has come up with a complete philosophy about how business can serve the community rather than exploit its customers. She has likened her ideas to those which motivated the Quakers, 'who ran successful businesses, made money because they offered honest products and treated their people decently, worked hard themselves, spent honestly, saved honestly, gave honest value for money, put back more than they took out and told no lies'.

Communism and the myth of an all-overseeing state bureaucracy may have been vanquished but at the moment the only replacement is capitalism, based as it is on self-interest, which is no more than a euphemism for greed and exploitation. The Earth's resources, however, are both finite and liable to exhaustion by mankind's inability to husband the environment, Capitalists will have to accept the need to share, rather than grab the largest portion, if we are to avoid endless warfare over the planet's dwindling stocks of raw materials.

In her recent autobiography, *Body and Soul*, Anita Roddick has defined the principles on which her business functions. 'In the Body Shop, the twin ideals of love and care touch everything we do, how we view our responsibilities, how we treat our staff, how we educate and communicate, how we relate to the community and the environment. When we invited our staff to write a charter that would codify our core values, the word "care" cropped up time and time again.' The firm trains its employees to realise their own potential rather than to simply sell more products and offers seminars on such subjects as urban survival, community action and drug abuse.

This is not to suggest that Prince Charles and Anita Roddick are closet Pagans, but to stress that Aquarian thinking is steadily reaching those who have the potential not only to provide a lead but also to create an atmosphere in which Paganism may be able to fill a spiritual vacuum. When the Aquarian revolution comes it will not be with guns, but rather from within the minds of the people, who will make their desires known. When that time comes the old religious sites will be reoccupied peacefully by the tribe, carrying flowers and moving on to Salisbury Plain behind their rainbow banners. This is no fantasy but will draw on the same collective force which smashed down the Berlin Wall. Those who practise the Craft in many countries around the world see a growing recognition of their beliefs and are convinced that Wicca has a role to play in the age of change. Pagan views are becoming increasingly aligned with those held by wide sections of the public.

Looking into the future, Janet and Stewart Farrar, who represent mainstream Wicca, believe the Craft is in tune with the times because of the emphasis it places on the development of psychic abilities. They predict that *homo sapiens* is on the threshold of an evolutionary leap in his psychic functioning, 'comparable with the leap that came about with the development of Ego-consciousness. This leap will be more compressed in time, and even more far-reaching in its consequences than the earlier leap. The time always produces the thinkers necessary for its consummation; and it may be that Gardner, when he pushed the Craft into the daylight, was in his own way arriving as punctually on the evolutionary scene as Freud, Jung, Copernicus and Einstein did in theirs.' To those illustrious names one could well add Martin Luther King, Bob Dylan, Bob Geldof, and Wally Hope.

The wider Pagan movement has always lacked a cohesive philosophy, although it has a common spiritual base anchored to the concept of the Earth as Mother. The witches, on the other hand, have many of the skills which would equip them to form a natural priesthood, akin to the Druids of old, serving as healers, leaders of ritual and as the guardians of the spiritual heritage of the tribes. This brings with it the danger of the formation of a new closed caste imposing its rule upon the followers. Doreen Valiente, a very wise witch and one whose intuitive writing has brought so many people into contact with Wiccan values, saw this very clearly: 'As the spiritual impetus behind the coming Age of Aquarius grows stronger, many institutions are changing as people begin to question the basic ideas upon which they are founded. Witchcraft is no exception to this process. Already, many young witches are questioning the old coven structure with its degrees and its requirements of secrecy. The idea of self-initiation would have been considered outrageous many years ago. Today witches ask, "Why not? Whose permission do we need to worship the Old Gods and celebrate the ritual occasions?" I think this is a fair question. A priestly hierarchy can become a power structure which is eventually concerned more with its own prestige than with anything else.'

Valiente qualified these strictures by stating that she did not believe that a priestly hierarchy would endure for long among the followers of the Old Religion, which she sees as: '. . . a happy, constructive religion, and what we now call magic will be a part of it. It will be involved with nature and the whole biosphere of our planet. It will be in communication with Mother Earth and with the changing seasons and the elements of life. It will take its stand against greed, cruelty and social injustice. Its rituals will have colour, music and dancing but also quiet times of meditation and healing for mind and body. It will help every man to be his own High Priest and every woman to be her own High Priestess. It will be part of the Aquarian Age.'

Those who regard themselves as Wiccans and Pagans firmly believe that there will be a place for religion in the future and that it will be based on individual freedom, love, and care for the planet. There will not be a priestly hierarchy, but certain gifted individuals will fulfil that role by popular accord rather than as a right gained by passing examinations. They also firmly believe that the nations of the world will be forced to disarm and that economic growth as a panacea will be seen for the fraud that it is. The tribes will move back to reclaim the land and grow what they need, while others will spread out into the Third World to tame the deserts and bring food to the hungry. During this process the religious bigots will finally be exposed by their own followers, whether in Belfast, Rome, Teheran or Tel Aviv. Only then will the God and the Goddess return to dwell among human beings in love and harmony.

Many new ideas are stirring in the Pagan world as believers attempt to come to terms with two competing trends. On the one hand, there is the need to combat the rise in attacks from Christian fundamentalist organizations; on the other, the need to organize in order to cope with increased public interest in Paganism. To deal with the threat posed by the fundamentalists the proprietor of a well-known occult supply shop in Leeds, whose premises have been fire-bombed, has formed the Sorcerer's Apprentice Fighting Fund, dedicated to collecting information about such incidents and countering negative publicity. There is also the Pagan Anti-defamation League, and the Pagan Federation has started actively to campaign for a positive media image.

This can only be achieved when more Pagans are prepared to defend their beliefs openly rather than leave the field open to a hard core of self-publicists.

The roughest problem faced by Pagans is undoubtedly that of future structure. There are still a great many Pagans, especially members of the more traditional Wiccan covens, who resist any movement towards a more open viewpoint. Some fear that public exposure might threaten their jobs, while others prefer the 'secret society' atmosphere and almost relish the thought of persecution. As the essence of Pagan thought is anti-dogmatic, and many believers love the freedom that this entails, discussions about forming a 'church' are anathema. In the United States, however, there are a number of Wiccan groupings which are recognized as churches, conferring charitable status and freedom from certain forms of taxation.

Another recent field of controversy concerns the Pagan priesthood and the need for a ministry. The supporters of a Pagan ministry feel that a Pagan should not be deprived of the comforts of religion when in hospital, near death or even in prison.

Wiccans believe that initiation itself confers membership of a priesthood, but this ignores the problem of ensuring an overall standard. The Fellowship of Isis offers ordination to suitably qualified individuals who are entitled to the call themselves 'reverend'. The Pagan Federation has been discussing the formation of a list of 'accredited' persons who can act as ministers, but as yet no clear consensus has emerged upon which such accreditation could be founded. What is clear is that the Pagan movement, regardless of how splintered it may appear to be, is seriously thinking about becoming recognized as a religion. There is, of course no reason why it should not be, provided that sufficient number of believers can agree on a common set of tenets to form a 'creed'. The prospect of Pagan assemblies in the local school might send shivers of apprehension down certain spines, but many Pagans feel that they should have the same right of access as anybody else.

However one may regard such beliefs as Paganism and Witchcraft, they nevertheless exist, do no apparent harm and are obviously here to stay. They satisfy the spiritual aspirations of an increasing section of the community and, with their basis in Celtic mysticism, strike a chord in the group soul of many a Briton.

❦ Suggestions ❦ for Further Reading

A full bibliography of the occult sciences would be way beyond the scope of this book. Listed below is a selection of those works which I feel have a direct bearing on the subjects dealt with in the preceding chapters and which have been written sincerely.

Adler, M.
Drawing Down the Moon. Beacon Press (USA), 1986.

Ashcroft-Nowicki, Dolores.
The Tree of Ecstasy. Aquarian Press, 1991.

Buckland, Raymond.
The Tree. Weiser (USA), 1974.

Carr-Gomm, Philip.
The Elements of the Druid Tradition. Element Books, 1991.

Conway, David.
Secret Wisdom. Jonathan Cape, 1985.
Magic. An Occult Primer. Aquarian Press, 1988.

Crowley, Vivienne.
  Wicca. The Aquarian Press, 1989.

Farrar, Janet and Stewart.
  The Witches' Way. Hale, 1984.
  The Witches' Goddess. Hale, 1987.
  The Witches' God. Hale, 1989.
  Eight Sabbats for Witches. Hale, 1981.

Green, Marian.
  The Path through the Labyrinth. Element Books, 1988.
  The Gentle Arts of Aquarian Magic. Aquarian Press, 1987.
  The Elements of Natural Magic. Element Books, 1989.
  Magic for the Aquarian Age. Aquarian Press, 1983.

Hope, Murry.
  The Psychology of Healing. Element Books, 1989.
  The Psychology of Ritual. Element Books, 1988.

Hough, Peter.
  Witchcraft. A Strange Conflict. Lutterworth Press, 1991.

Hughes, Penethorne.
  Witchcraft. Longmans, 1952.

Matthews, Caitlin (ed).
  Voices of the Goddess. Aquarian Press, 1989.

Regardie, Israel.
  The Foundations of Practical Magic. Aquarian Press, 1982.

Starhawk.
  The Spiral Dance. Harper and Row, (USA), 1979.

Valiente, Doreen.
  The Rebirth of Witchcraft. Hale, 1989.
  Witchcraft for Tomorrow. Hale, 1978.
  Natural Magic. Hale, 1975.

Warren-Clarke, Ly.
  The Way of the Goddess. Prism Press, 1987.

Wilson, Colin.
  Mysteries. Granada, 1985.
  The Occult. Granada, 1979.

❦ Useful Addresses ❦

The Pagan Federation,
BM Box 7097,
London WC1N 3XX.
(The prime source of contact for those wishing further information about Wicca and Paganism).

The Order of Brighid
91 Reigate Road
West Worthing,
Sussex.
(A non-secret Pagan group offering training and preparation for priest/esshood).

The Fellowship of Isis,
Clonegal Castle,
Enniscorthy,
Eire.

Pagan Animal Rights,
23 Highfield South,
Rock Ferry,
Wirral,
Merseyside.

The Pagan Hospice and Funeral Trust,
BM Box 3337
London WC1N 3XX

The Order of Bards, Ovates and Druids,
260 Kew Road,
Richmond,
Surrey, TW9 3EG
(Offers courses in the Druid tradition).

Paganlink Network,
25 East Hill,
Dartford.
Kent.
(Acts through regional members as a contact network putting Pagans in touch with each other).

❦ Index ❦

199

versions of, 6, 43
women, attraction for,
  78
working tools, 114–15
Wiccaning, 126
Wilson, Colin, 69
Windsor Great Park
  festival, 47
Witchcraft
  child abuse, allegations
    of, 7
  Elizabethan England, in,
    20
  ethical responsibility, 70
  moral initiative in, 55
  Murray, theories of, 35
  repeal of statutes
    against, 35
  Satanism, no relation
    to, 6
  sociology of, 131
  statutes, repeal of, 6
  traditional, pockets of, 6
  United States, in, 41
  women's rights move-
    ment, benefiting
    from, 41
Witches
  activities, programmes
    of, 117–18
  beliefs, concealing,
    135–6
  children, approach to,
    141
  Civil War and
    Commonwealth,
    persecution during,
    21
  dancing, 63–4

death ritual, 127–9
healing, 142–3
herbal remedies, 143
independence, 117
jewellery, 112
marks, identification by,
  20
meditation, 125
naked, working, 108–11
own personality, com-
  ing to terms with,
  110
power, raising, 63
Protestants destroying,
  19
pseudonyms, using,
  135–6
robes, 111–12
self-publicists, 136
services, not charging
  for, 134
sexual perversion,
  accusation of, 161
Shakespeare's view of,
  21–2
typical, 133
wedding, 127, 155
work, 107
working, 124–5
working alone, 88
younger faction, 133
Woodman, W.R., 31

Yeats, W.B., 32
Yoga, 167
Youth culture, explosion
  of, 47
Yule, 150–2